T0129630

Finding Her Voice

WILLOMINO PEARL

BALBOA.
PRESS
A DIVISION OF HAY HOUSE

Balboa Press books may be ordered through booksellers or by contacting:

Balboa Press
A Division of Hay House
1663 Liberty Drive
Bloomington, IN 47403
www.balboapress.com
1 (877) 407-4847

Because of the dynamic nature of the Internet, any web addresses or links contained in this book may have changed since publication and may no longer be valid. The views expressed in this work are solely those of the author and do not necessarily reflect the views of the publisher, and the publisher hereby disclaims any responsibility for them.

The author of this book does not dispense medical advice or prescribe the use of any technique as a form of treatment for physical, emotional, or medical problems without the advice of a physician, either directly or indirectly. The intent of the author is only to offer information of a general nature to help you in your quest for emotional and spiritual well-being. In the event you use any of the information in this book for yourself, which is your constitutional right, the author and the publisher assume no responsibility for your actions.

Any people depicted in stock imagery provided by Getty Images are models, and such images are being used for illustrative purposes only. Certain stock imagery © Getty Images.

Print information available on the last page.

ISBN: 978-1-9822-2712-8 (sc)
ISBN: 978-1-9822-2713-5 (e)

Balboa Press rev. date: 05/15/2019

CONTENTS

Chapter 1   Mother's Death 1

Chapter 2   Remembering 3

Chapter 3 9

Chapter 4   Memories 11

Chapter 5 14

Chapter 6   Her First Boyfriends 16

Chapter 7   Job 20

Chapter 8   18 22

Chapter 9   Mother finding Compassion 24

Chapter 10   Life after 18 26

Chapter 11   Moving Back 30

Chapter 12   Miserable Life 34

Chapter 13   Making Decisions 37

Chapter 14   Moving On Their Own 40

Chapter 15   Home with Baby 43

Chapter 16   Eddie 45

Chapter 17   Their Business 49

Chapter 18   Sister Gatherings 51

Chapter 19   Motor Cycle Group 54

Chapter 20   Incorporation 58

Chapter 21 61

Chapter 22   Too Close for Comfort 65

Chapter 23   First Grandson 70

Chapter 24   Eddie's Friends 72

Chapter 25 75
Chapter 26 Working for Mother 77
Chapter 27 Alone 78
Chapter 28 80
Chapter 29 83
Chapter 30 85
Chapter 31 89
Chapter 32 91
Chapter 33 One night Stand 93
Chapter 34 Trial Trip 96
Chapter 35 Secret Admirer 98
Chapter 36 Letter 100
Chapter 37 Eviction Notice 102
Chapter 38 Truth 105
Chapter 39 Packing 108
Chapter 40 Learning How Too Cope 110
Chapter 41 Eight Years Later 113
Chapter 42 Finding Madelyn 115

To All that Read This Book 119

CHAPTER 1
Mother's Death

As her sisters, brother and Madelyn stood over her Mother as she lay dying only one tear rolled down Madelyn's cheek. It was finally over. She died on June sixth nineteen- ninety five.

Her Mother was diagnosed with cancer in February of that same year. She brought her seven children together and asked her children to take care of her while she died at home. Their Father died at home of Cancer also, only his was of the lung and bone. Madelyn's Mother's was a tumor on the outside wall of her stomach possibly from her ovaries.

At that time Madelyn was confused about the feeling she had for her Mother. Her Mother made Madelyn's life miserable. She still loved her because she was her Mother. She still helped take care of her because that was the right thing to do.

Deep down inside of her though, she couldn't wait for her to die. She would no longer have to hear her criticize her for everything she did. Little did she know that Madelyn would carry her voice in her head for a very long time after her Mother's death!

Madelyn stayed through the day and Sister Elaine during the night. They both had jobs for a while. Madelyn's was with a Cleaning Company that she soon quit because the owners were recovering addicts who played one cleaning team against the other. Madelyn didn't like those kinds of games so soon she quit.

She could at least stay with her mother longer through the day. They always had disagreements about different things until she went to bed. Her Mother still had that spunk. Madelyn did what she did best, cleaned and exercised and watched TV waiting for Elaine to get there so she could leave. She hated being there. Their Mother wanted to die twelve years earlier when their father died. At first she was ok with father's death. She said she'd have more money. Soon her money didn't make her happy she was lonely. She started driving but that didn't last long. She was afraid. Then she became dependent on Elaine and Madelyn to take her to the grocery store and to the Doctors office.

After their Father died she just kept saying she wanted to die after the loneliness set in. She had a heart attack and had by-pass surgery but before while getting ready to go to surgery she kissed everyone. Madelyn's Mother thought for sure she was going to die during surgery but God had other plans for her. She had more work to do before she left. Madelyn's Mother lived twelve more years after that heart attack and by-pass surgery.

CHAPTER 2
Remembering

The first memory Madelyn had of her Mother was of her carrying Madelyn up the long hill which was the drive way. It hurts she remembers. Mother carried her side ways and each step on the rocky drive way sent pain into her side. Madelyn couldn't wait to get to the top so she would put her down so she could walk the rest of the way. I guess Mother thought she was to slow so she carried her.

Their house was huge. It had to be, Madelyn had five sisters and one brother. The house had a kitchen. Sitting room, good living room, for entertainment purposes, a hall and an upstairs with four bedrooms. They had no bathroom. There was an outside toilet. The heat was a coal furnace. No heat upstairs except for a small gas heater which only got used when it was bitterly cold out. The one register that was in the hall way upstairs was there so the heat from downstairs would rise up though the register and help heat the upstairs.

They used pots, thunder mugs as they were also called. Pots that they peed and pooped in during the night and Madelyn was the master carrier of the pots. They had a little one for the smaller girls and she also carried it to. Madelyn remembers thinking who poops and pees that much during the night? A family that size had a lot to eliminate during the night hours.

Madelyn remembers one time she spilled the pot. It ran down the register grids and into the kitchen below. It was a mess. She cried during the whole cleaning. Nobody helped. Her Mother just kept telling her to do it right or there would be consequences. The poop got stuck in the grids of the register and there were no rubber gloves in the house so Madelyn had to dig into the grids with her fingers to dig the poop out. It was one lesson she will never forget.

In the summer carrying those pots she would step on the bees that were on the clover flowers in their yard. There were many time that she would throw the little pot up in the air after stepping on a bee. She'd cry and someone would come out and take the stinger out of her foot. It happened at least fifty or sixty times during the years she carried the pot.

They had no running water. There was a pump in the kitchen that they used to wash dishes and to bath in from a cistern. They caught rain water to wash their hair and carried water from the spring to drink. They were paid one penny a gallon and got a raise as they got older to two cents per gallon. Their brother could move faster and carry more so made more money than the girls.

They bathed in a galvanized tub in the middle of the kitchen all using the same water. The water had to be heated on the stove in big kettles and it took a while to heat the water and at the end of it all it turned cold before the last child was bathed.

Madelyn's Mother was strict. What was she saying she was downright mean!

Madelyn's Mother demanded respect from her children. If she didn't get it, they got it and it wasn't respect. They were beaten with belts sometimes buckle end up. With boards with holes in the end which made it hurt that much more. Hit in the head with metal gravy spoons. If you cried with your mouth open and (who doesn't) you had a bar of soap appear out of nowhere scrapped on your teeth. It was horrible punishment. Most of the time the anger came from nowhere it seemed. If one piece of candy was missing or something was broken, or something wasn't done right or someone didn't fess up to the crime at hand they were all punished and still no one confessed to the crime.

The punishment was to instill fear. It worked for Madelyn. She was afraid of everything. Afraid to do anything wrong. She was afraid to come home one minute late. If anyone of her sisters were punished Madelyn remembers how she stood back and cried for that sister or her brother. She was afraid to speak up for her fear overtook her and she stood and said nothing for fear she'd be punished to. She hated her Mother but she also knew it was a sin to hate anyone especially your Mother. She didn't know how to feel. She just kept those feeling buried deep inside. She wrote on paper but tore it up for fear of someone reading what she wrote. She had only writing or going to the tree on the hill to let out her hatred and frustrations.

Mother had some unexplained behavior. Mental illness was the only explanation Madelyn could think of. Madelyn remembers when Father was dying he didn't want anyone to touch him. He said it hurt. Her Mother called her over and said watch this. She was at the foot of the bed and was edging her hand towards Father's foot he kept saying "don't, please don't." She hadn't even touched him but he just kept saying it hurts. She laughed.

She had some good qualities to. She taught us to clean... Really well. She said if you can't do it right the first time then just don't do it. That stuck with Madelyn. Madelyn knew then that was how she'd get some attention. Something that she longed for. Someone to love her.

Madelyn's Mother's words played a big role in Madelyn's life. Always being criticized for the work she did in the house. It was half assed as her Mother said. "You will never amount to nothing" "you are dumb". "Stupid".

Madelyn had a place to go so that she could just stop thinking about how dumb she was and the inside pain that she felt. She'd go to the tree. The tree was in the woods. She'd go to the rope swing and swing out over the hill. If the limb would break then she'd be in the neighbor back yard with broken bones no less. It would be a hard fall... Maybe she'd even die. Something that she started thinking about.

Why was she here? Why didn't anyone love her? What was life all about? Madelyn went to church. Her Father was the Pasture of the church. She believed that she had to do everything right that the church taught her or she'd go to hell. Always ask for forgiveness. She did all those things but yet no one loved her.

Madelyn was that little girl that didn't have a voice. She couldn't speak up to say what she wanted. She was afraid... Of everything and everyone. No one had anything nice to say to her or about her. She was stuck in a world where no one seen her or cared about her. She was dumb, she was ugly, and she had to stay hidden. The one character that everyone noticed about her was her smile.

They were strangers though. Her face turned bright red from being embarrassed by the smile and the attention she so craved but was embarrassed by.

She got attention sometimes, whenever her Mother couldn't get a confession out of one her siblings when something was wrong or one piece of candy was gone or something was broken. Everyone got a beaten. Still there was no confession.

As the little Madelyn got older she started school. She walked with the older sister about a mile. The class room was large and there were so many students. Class ranged from first grade to seventh grade all in one room and there were only two teachers.

What was she doing here? It was a mandatory place she had to be. At least she was away from her home. She struggled with learning and homework. Madelyn didn't understand the work. She couldn't stay focused. Reading was the worst and comprehending what she read. If Madelyn was called upon she was so embarrassed her face turned bright red and everyone looked at her. She just wanted the floor to suck her up.

After school her friend would come to visit and her friend being a good friend helped her do her chores so they could go to the tree swing or go climb a trees. This was her best friend who she loved and spent a lot of time just pretending. They'd go to the train tussles and climb down in between the rail road ties to the concrete barriers below and just look at the crick travel by far below them. It was kind of dangerous but that didn't scare them. They just had fun.

As Madelyn got older she inherited her brother's paper route. It was good and that Christmas she got her first bike so she could deliver papers. Some of her customers though didn't want to pay and they still expected to get their paper. She had a hard time telling them they weren't going to get a paper so she'd sneak by the house so she didn't have to tell them. Confrontations were something Madelyn had a tough time with. She couldn't confront her Mother or give an opinion or she might be busted in the face for talking back or she'd be shammed by her Father's talk.

One day the customer waited on her and asked why they weren't getting their paper. She told them they had to pay first. They knew she wasn't strong in demanding her money so they intimidated her by sicing their dog on her. The dog bit her on the foot as she sat on her bike. She just peddled off. Her way was to get away, flight not fight. She hated the fighting.

Another incident that happened Madelyn was walking to deliver her papers when she noticed that one of the neighborhood young adults was following her. The hair stood up on the back of her neck when he followed her into a secluded area where the railroad bridge crossed the crick. She kept delivering the papers along the row before the bridge. He kept following. She thought, he could be going to the little store along the row but when she crested the hill and in her small voice she turned and looked at him and said "Are you following me?" This was a neighbor who had gotten older and was quiet and creepy. He looked at her and said "NO." She took him at his word and kept on walking over the hill crest and towards the bridge. As she stepped onto the foot bridge she was suddenly attacked for behind. She could never scream out loud before but the voice came and she screamed and he dropped her and he ran one way and she ran the other. As she got to the other side of the bridge she was shaking with the kind of fear she had never experienced before. She looked back to see if he was still following, he wasn't but what she saw next was something she would never forget. The whole experience she wouldn't forget anyhow but what she saw was disturbing. Her attacker held something in his hand and he shook it at her. What was that? It looked like a bat. She'd never seen anything like it in her young life.

She was so afraid of what just happened to her but she knew she had to deliver the papers not a one could get lost they were all accounted for. She was like the mail carriers who delivered the mail in rain shine or snow the papers were going to be delivered. She feared what her Mother would do if Mother had to pay for the papers Madelyn lost. All the papers were delivered before she went home.

She entered crying telling her parents what had happened an hour before. Her Mother called the neighbor. The neighbor denied the allegations and defended her son that he had thumbed his way to town an hour ago. Madelyn's Mother told Madelyn "he was thumbing to town at that time". She didn't believe Madelyn. She didn't care. It was all swept under the rug never to be spoken of again. It was a week or two later that her attacker raped a young women. In Madelyn's silence she said to herself and to them silently of course, "I told you so". The pain was buried deep inside and she wondered who would ever protect her from the outside world if her parents didn't, who then?

That ended Madelyn's career as the "Paper Girl".

CHAPTER 3

M adelyn wanted to find out who she was in the coming years as
she grew older. She asked God one time to take her away she
wanted to leave this so called life of misery. Why did she have this
life? She couldn't wait to grow up. She'd find someone to love her. Her
mother didn't. She tried so hard to get her Mother to love her. She
cleaned for her as well as she could, so proud of her own work. Her
Mother never complimented her, never said how proud she was of her.
Madelyn assumed the job was a half done job.

Madelyn had such low self-esteem. She tried to shrink down
to nothing or just disappear into the wall. She couldn't look into
anyone's face. No eye contact. Embarrassed to non-existence if anyone
noticed her.

Her Father and Mother did that to her. They imprinted on her
at a very young age. Her Father never beat the children only once
that Madelyn could remember. It was when Mother had him talk to
the children, they were shamed with the "TALK" from their Father.
Shamed into looking at the floor so if Madelyn was spoken to by
anyone that's what she did… It was so hurtful looking back. It's hard to
believe she was so beaten down. Compared to now, how much wisdom
she collected through the years about herself. She had good qualities no

matter what she'd done. She just had to believe in herself and squash the fears and shine but when you're little and you're being told over and over all negative things about yourself you begin to believe that untruth. "You're stupid you'll never amount to anything, you can't do anything right, you're a total screw up, you're fat, you're ugly when you cry." Madelyn believed it all.

She understood that her Mother didn't know any better. Her Mother was raised with that belief about herself. So how can Madelyn blame her for how she treated Madelyn? Unbelievable? Deep down in her soul she believes now that she chose this life that she chose to be with these parents and her whole life growing up was miserable. Madelyn didn't understand then that this whole life thing is all about lessons and forgiveness and "LOVE".

Madelyn carried the pain of growing up for many years. She couldn't move forward with her life. Always looking for someone to find her attractive or some attention of any kind. Her grades were average and she thought that anything she did was not good enough.

In grade school she had abusive teachers. The one teacher would slap her on the back as she stood at the chalkboard trying to figure out the problem at hand. She guessed that the teacher tried to slap the answer out of you. No tears though. It was just embarrassing.

Madelyn remembers that there were fights all the time in their house. They were physical fights between her sisters and brother, sisters and sisters. If there weren't then it was her Mother that was hitting or fighting with one of them. She remembers one incident where her Mother almost killed her brother over a broken window. Her Mother couldn't stop beating him. She beat him until he fell into the wall and beat his head against the wall then when he fell to the ground she kicked him. He was too weak to fight back so their Father stepped in to stop her from killing him. Madelyn just stood and cried afraid to step in or her Mother would surely kill her to. Her Mother had no control over her anger. She did not like to be disrespected. She demanded respect.

CHAPTER 4
Memories

Madelyn's Father had two jobs. When he wasn't working he was sleeping or reading the bible. He was a religious man. He was one of the Pastors of the church they belonged to.

Her Father never hugged them or very seldom did only at bedtime when they were very young but as young teens that was never something he did.

Mother told them that their Father didn't hug them because he was afraid he would be accused of molestation. At that time Madelyn wondered what that meant. She didn't have a clue. She'd find out later in life though.

She remembers going to church and her father would hug her cousin. He'd kiss her on the cheek and they'd hug and converse about who knows what. She always thought how jealous she was of her. What's the difference in hugging them or Father hugging his cousin. He didn't trust them, or was it Mother who put that idea in his head? Why did Mother hate them?

At times Madelyn just wanted to die. She'd be so angry because Mother would tell them on Friday after school that if they would wash and wax the floors on their hands and knees and make their beds clean their rooms she'd give them a quarter to go to the skating rink, about half to a mile away from the house. Sometimes at the end of the clean she'd say Madelyn and her sister waxed the hair to the floors so they couldn't go. Madelyn was the one who waxed the floors. Elaine scrubbed.

She'd go to her room and cry and say to God just take me away. Kill me right now. Is this what life is about to be constantly punished be in fear and pain. She just didn't want to be there! That's probably when she started wondering about who she was and why was she on this earth what purpose did she have here. She was who she was... Not her sister not the neighbor she was Madelyn, that person who was so hated and so abused and so unhappy and scared. All created in her mind by the life she lived in that house. She could only see the pain. She couldn't see the happy times. She feared that when there were happy times that she'd do something to mess it up so she was cautious about how she reacted to even positive days.

Knowing what she's learned today she has a hard time believing she chose that life before she left heaven. She created a lot of Karma in the lives before she came back so she must have had a lot of lessons to learn to go through the hell she went through. It was the belief that she was worthless and would never amount to anything which created a lot of grief in her adult life. She did not love herself. How could anyone love her? Her own parents didn't love her so who would? She was just another mouth to feed.

Mother definitely kept them busy. They scrubbed walls down at least two times a year painted at least once a year. Mother never complimented them if they did a good job. Madelyn just assumed it was half assed.

Mother was always pregnant it seemed. Madelyn didn't know what was wrong though she just knew Mother would be sick a lot. Throwing up and then there would be another sister to take care of.

The sister's had to get up in the morning and get that new sister up and make sure they had a diaper change and set her in the high chair and make sure they had her shoes and socks on. Then give them something to eat.

The sisters had cloth diapers and plastic pants over the diaper. That was a mess... full of urine and poop...Madelyn had to rinse the poop out in a bucket of water.

Madelyn escaped to the tree a lot. She'd dreamed that she would have a family but never beat her children or make them do any house work. Madelyn found out later that that promise about not making them do house work was one that she should have never made.

Mother had her so brow beaten. Madilyn's personality being the way it was and her backing down from her Mother. She deemed herself a coward. She couldn't stand up to people when they walked on her and if they abused her, she thought she deserved it. She believed she did something wrong.

Madelyn remembering how strict her Mother was and her Mother didn't think or ask questions before she punished her children. Madelyn left her bike at the foot of the hill one day after delivering papers, She walked up the hill and her sister Elaine started on her about doing the dishes so Madelyn started doing the dishes when suddenly her Mother come through the door and came after her with a board. Her younger sister came across the road from the playground to get Madelyn's bike which was sitting at the foot of the hill and almost got hit by a car.

That was Madelyn's fault... why? Because she didn't bring the bike up the hill. Listen... pushing that bike up the hill after delivering the papers was hard. She was tired and to be screamed at to do the dishes as soon as she walked through the door then Mother coming after her with a board and beating her on the fronts of my legs was just something she didn't think she brought on herself. Why... Why... Why...?????

CHAPTER 5

One of her friends, Billy. He was adopted from a family of 13 or 14 kids. They were friends and played baseball together rode bikes and swung on the rope swing. He was Cool... Until one day when we got older and Billy and her grew apart. He started riding a go-cart around and he became very careless. He crossed a bridge and a car coming from the opposite direction hit him head on. He died that day. It was a shock to them all. This was her first encounter with death.

She started thinking about death. Where did a person go when they died? In church they were always taught that when you die if you were good you'd go to heaven but if you sinned you'd go to hell and burn forever. She wondered did Billy go to hell because he certainly wasn't doing anything good when he died.

Church was boring. She was made to get up early and go to church. She just wanted to sleep in. Sunday school she can barely remember what went on and then there was the preaching service. Really boring. The pastors where not very interesting. They couldn't hold her attention and she just prayed they'd hurry up and get done so she could go home and eat.

One Pastor in particular cried the whole sermon. He was touched by the Holy Spirit. As they say. The others were just as boring. She learned though. As she got older she remembered a lot of what the bible was about. Then it became important to her. She could understand what the parables meant then.

She wondered why her Mother's beating and some of the off the wall punishments weren't a sin. Her Father smoked cigarettes and that wasn't treating our body like a temple.

Why wasn't any of that a sin? She was afraid to be bad but apparently she was. She was afraid of everything except the woods. She loved the woods. They were peaceful and even made her smile. She'd pick the purple and white violets to take home to her Mother so her Mother would be happy and maybe even say thank you, you are such a good girl but that never happened. That she could remember anyhow. She just wanted to be loved.

CHAPTER 6
Her First Boyfriends

L ife moved on for her with the fear and beatings and the lessons. School was a hassle. She was not the cool kid. Her clothes were hand made and she wore the same clothes for three days and the same shoes for a year.

She was shy so she didn't make friends easily because she just wasn't out going enough. She couldn't carry on a friendship when she was limited to what she did or where she was allowed to go. Mother was strict. Who'd want to be Madelyn's friend anyway? She was awkward. She was stupid. She had no voice.

She was so shy and so unsure of herself ... saying the wrong thing, just being noticed she wanted to just be sucked up by the floor or disappear into the wood work.

She couldn't talk without saying the wrong things describing anything was so hard. She stuttered and didn't have a voice so she became was very quiet around people. She was seen but never heard. She was frightened of everything. She was laughed at for what, she don't even remember, Or was it all in her head?

Walking across the street in high school was embarrassing. She didn't know how to cross with the red and green lights. She was never taught. She dare not ask, that only showed them how stupid she was.

Madelyn tried to cross but almost got run over by a car and the guy yelled out "what the hell is the matter with you, you dumb ass, you trying to get killed"? She looked around to see all looking at her and she politely said that he was her uncle he was just teasing. Yea right, who believed that lie? There it was she was going to hell for lying. She just wanted to be sucked up by the cracks in the sidewalks.

As she got older things didn't change much. They were still beaten and still worked their butts off to keep them out of trouble.

School was a drag. Madelyn had a few friends but not many. She just couldn't wait to get out of school and be 18. Get away from Mother and Father.

She met her first serious boyfriend when she was a freshman in high school. He was a senior.

Mother was okay with it (SURPRISE). They didn't go anywhere except he came to the house and they sat and played board games. He was the first one to convince her to have sex. She was so scared and she thought she was pregnant even when he used two condoms. First experience and it was awful. It continued though. Madelyn thought she had to, to keep a boyfriend, someone that would give her the attention that she obviously wanted.

He graduated high school and joined the service. First love, and she was in love. She was really upset after he left.

They broke up after a few months. Madelyn needed the attention from another boyfriend so she wrote a Dear John letter to her boyfriend in the service. "Oh, the Dear John letter" was something the boyfriends in the service never wanted to get... She was interested in finding someone new. There wasn't another man in her life that loved her. Madelyn really didn't even know who she was. Just another girl who didn't have a clue what she was capable of. She was trying to find herself by getting a man to love her. She thought he would complete her as a person. Her thinking was she needed someone to love her unconditionally she didn't know that she needed to learn to love herself first.

Her self -esteem plummeted.

She started looking for another boyfriend and along came Eddie. He was definitely interested and she was also interested. So… the romance began. She was allowed to date. Her Mother and Father became friends with his parents and things progressed until after 2 years he cheated on her not once but two times and she forgave him but the second time was pretty hard. He compared her to her the other girl. She was fit and she had no love handles. Wow!! Madelyn was crushed. She already had no self-esteem and to hear that was a crash and burn. How could she change herself to suit his needs to make him love her?

She forgave him though. They continued on with their relationship. He was a junior and she was to. He was two years older than her because he was failed in lower grades for being left handed.

Out of the blue he decided to quit school and join the service. Why? They all knew she wasn't good with handling the boyfriend going to the service. She couldn't live without the boyfriend in her life. She tried though. He left. When he was about to graduate from boot camp Madelyn traveled to see him graduate with his parents. Eddie bought her an engagement ring in North Carolina and it was beautiful. She was so happy. Was this unconditional love?

Another story though when it came to telling her parents. She was only 16 and he was 18.

They were let's say…. not at all happy. She was too young and they did not approve.

She was just caught up in the moment. Let's say she was just so happy that someone loved her enough to buy this expensive ring and her self- esteem was through the roof.

That all lasted a grand total of about one year. Mother was on her about everything. "You'll never graduate from high school'. She was about to turn 18 and her Mother was still the controlling person who verbally beat her along with the physical beatings keeping her self -esteem as low as possible. She ran away from home shortly after a letter came in the mail from her boyfriend that told her Mother that if she didn't start treating Madelyn better that he was coming to take her away from the abuse. Her Mother became very angry when she read the letter. Madelyn's life became a living hell. Her Mother didn't understand the hurtful things she put her children through. The abuse became worse. Madelyn ran away. She stayed with a friend but her Mother found her. Her Mother and Father drove up to the house and told her if she didn't come home she was going to call the local police department and have her taken into custody. Madelyn didn't go home she ended up staying with her boyfriend's parents.

That didn't last long either. Everyone started talking about her to those parents and Eddie's Mother asked her to leave and when she left to leave the engagement ring on the night stand. Madelyn did what she was told. His Mother broke them up. Madelyn wasn't angry she deserved to be broken up with she blamed Eddie for writing the letter to her Mother. The things she wrote to him was private and he just caused a long chain of events to happen which ended in them breaking up.

CHAPTER 7

Job

Madelyn then decided to move in with her Mother again. She got a job at the town's ice cream store. They sold grilled cheese sandwiches, fish, fries, and hamburgers, and of course Ice cream to the students from the local school and the public.

Something started happening to Madelyn while she worked there. Her boss was a women and her husband owned the Ice cream shop. She started noticing that the male boss was passing through and he was rubbing Madelyn's butt as he passed. It made her feel uncomfortable but she passed it off as just accidental touching because the aisles were narrow behind the lunch bar. It just kept happening over and over though. She became so aware of the improper touching that she was afraid to go upstairs to the bathroom and that's where everyone clocked in. She was afraid he'd catch her alone. Then what would she do? She was already in that situation before when the man attacked her on the foot bridge. This was her boss and he had a mean wife.

She was such a nervous wreck she was afraid to go upstairs to look at the schedule for fear he'd come up. She just left after the shift. The next day she was scheduled to work and never went to work and was immediately fired for being a no show. She had to tell her Mother about being fired. She just told her that they didn't need her anymore. She couldn't tell her that her boss was inappropriately touching her. The last time nobody cared so, why would they this time?

CHAPTER 8

18

Madelyn coped an attitude. She was about to turn 18 and she became one of those kids that she thought she knew everything and nobody was going to tell her what to do. She started missing school or going in late for classes. She started going to the local Pizza shop where they sold beer. She didn't drink until she started running around with a girl let us say she didn't have a good reputation. They together started drinking. Madelyn wasn't so good at this task. She was definitely a light weight. She'd drink one beer and go outside and throw up.

The owner of the Pizza Place was four times her senior. He said he loved her. She thought that it was all innocent and they were just friends. He'd kiss her just lightly on the cheek. He told her all the time how beautiful she was and talked about taking her to Australia. Of course Madelyn thought he was just a nice old man and didn't think too much of his passing kiss on the cheek. One evening he just out and out laid a kiss on her lips and put his hand on her breast. Man what a surprise that was. She then knew how stupid she was for believing he was just a nice old man. He was just another old pervert looking to molest a young girl.

Madelyn stopped her bad behavior when she met a man. He was

her brother's friend and he only lived around the hill from where she lived. She met him at the Pizza House and he seemed interested in her. She became interested also enough to go out on a date with him. He had his own car and she was eighteen now. He was six years older than her.

Under the roof of her Mother she still had rules and anger issues with her Mother. Her Mother didn't like her boyfriend. Her Mother was out spoken and said mean things about his family in front of him. His Mother was a holy roller in the church at the foot of our hill in the neighborhood. His Uncle stole all the lumber to build his house from the railroad where he had worked. She didn't like Jerry at all. He was good looking and all but he was too old for Madelyn and he was a drinker.

Madelyn didn't know too much about drinking only that she had done some of it while she was being unruly and really didn't like the way it made her feel. "Sick."

She remembers her Uncle and Aunt coming to the house and they brought alcohol and Mother never let them put it in the refrigerator. They sat it at their feet or if it was winter they sat it on the porch. They drank the whole time they visited. They seemed normal so what was the big deal about drinking.

Little did she know what kind of world she was getting into in her future!

CHAPTER 9
Mother finding Compassion

Finally, Mother and Father decided to invest in a bathroom and do away with the "POTS." They also got a new furnace. No more coal. They got an oil furnace instead.

To start out with everything had to be cleaned that meant scrubbing all the walls down and fresh paint to rid the house of all the coal residue from years of burning coal.

Madelyn had to do all her chores before her and Jerry could go out on a date. She was in love with Jerry. He spoke to her like she was a person and not look away when he spoke to her. She loved him so much that they started having intimate relation. Her Mother just kept saying if you get pregnant we are giving your baby away. She didn't know they were having sex she was just guessing. Madelyn denied ever having done that. She was afraid her Mother would make her stop seeing him all together and Madelyn was to in love to have to give him up. Any how she thought, she was 18 what could her Mother do to stop her. Mother antagonized her all the time. She'd say now that you have a boyfriend you'll never graduate from high school. She knew Jerry wasn't going anywhere like the other two who joined the service because Jerry had already been in the service and was out now.

One day my sister came home drunk, crying and looked at our

Mother and said and don't say a word. She went upstairs and Madelyn became afraid. Mother hated being disrespected and she was certain Elaine had just disrespected her coming home drunk and speaking to her in the manner that she did.

Madelyn remembered when Elaine came home from a ride with her boyfriend and it was about a week before she turned 16. The rule was they were not to get in the car with their boyfriend until they turned 16. Mother was so angry that she took a belt and started yelling at her and beating her with the belt buckle. The next day Elaine had belt buckle marks all over her even on her neck. Mother had no control and again Madelyn had failed her sister she was afraid to step in for fear she'd be next.

Mother started up the steps and in Madelyn's small voice she said "Please don't beat her." Elaine just had caught her boyfriend cheating on her and she confronted him after she got drunk then came home.

It stayed quiet upstairs. She didn't know what was going on but she was crying like it was happening to her. Her Mother found compassion and only held her as she cried. That made Madelyn cry even harder. She had never seen her mother have such compassion.

CHAPTER 10

Life after 18

M adelyn visited the tree on the hill whenever she got a chance. By then the tree was struck by lightning or just old age dropped it over and there was no more tree swing. She was older then so just climbing up on the tree itself was enough to keep her from going crazy in that house. She loved that tree and to this day she thinks about that old tree and how much of a good friend she was to her.

Graduation came and went and Madelyn moved out. Her oldest sister let her move in with her and her husband. Her husband was a drinking partner for Jerry though.

She didn't know much about drinking. Father only got drunk once that she knew of. Mother every once in- awhile bought a 6 pack and got drunk but always ended up throwing up after wards.

She soon found out what it was like to live with an alcoholic. Jerry drank a lot. They'd go to his Mom's house and he'd sneak into the cupboard and find whiskey and would drink a shot or two. His Mom would come in and scold him. She didn't want her husband to find out. That was her Mafia husband. At least that is what Jerry told Madelyn.

Jerry didn't come home a lot. He'd stay out all night and come home in the morning and say he passed out and couldn't drive. She couldn't understand that. What happened to the "man" she thought was going to be her forever and love her unconditionally.

They got an opportunity to move to another city. Jerry could work in a factory with a friend and they could live with Jerry's ex- girlfriend and her husband (Jerry's friend). Oh great, now she was getting away from his drinking partner and that meant an opportunity to start fresh again.

First, Madelyn's sister made her call Mother and tell her she was going to move away. Why? She was 18. In that state you had to be 21 before you were considered an adult. At 18 you still had to have your Mother's consent to get married. But Madelyn was pregnant!

That same old fear came over her but she stepped into her power and called and said" Mother I'm moving to Bakersfield with Jerry". Mother said no you're not or I'm calling the truant officer. She told her go ahead that when she went before the judge he'd find out she was pregnant and he'd marry them anyway. So, the cat was out of the bag. She told her Mother she was pregnant.

I guess Madelyn moving away with Jerry would be better than being married to him by a judge. Mother didn't want her marrying Jerry for sure.

They moved. They lived with Jerry's ex Tiffany and her husband Don. Don was a good guy. He looked Madelyn in the face and talked to her like a real person. He was genuinely concerned with her welfare. They were good people but it was obvious she ruled the roost. Everything was just so… so… and in order. Clothes folded to a tee. They had one child at the time.

Madelyn and Jerry stayed with them until they found their own place. (Thank the lord). She wanted to start their own life together... alone.

Ended up they moved in with another friend, Dick. That was Jerry's friend too.

Ugh!! Were they ever going to get a break?

Eventually they got their break. Dick went back to his home town. Madelyn's brother Eric and his wife at the time were living downstairs. Brother and sister weren't very close. Childhood memories kept them from being friends. Eric's wife was insulting and was hurtful with the things she said out loud to Madelyn "You're a little on the chunky side and Jerry reminds me of my ex, always drunk. Then she'd laugh with that toothy smile she had.

Jerry was not a very good husband. He needed time away from Madelyn apparently. He stayed out all night. He worked three shifts. He wouldn't go to work half the time on midnight and when he did he didn't go. Jerry went out drinking and came home drunk, or he'd go out drinking in the morning and come home and couldn't go to work afternoon shift because he was hung over. Day shift he couldn't get up and go half the time. They did nothing but fight over his drinking.

Madelyn threatened to leave but never did. She even packed and left, but came back. He never asked her to stay. She was afraid to be alone and go back to Mother. She didn't want to hear "I told you so". Madelyn hated to think her Mother was right about her choice of husband. She wouldn't have made that choice if she hadn't tried so hard to get away from her abuser, only to step into another abusive situation only this one was an abuse she didn't recognize as abuse.

She didn't know why but she thought if they were married things would get better. The conditioned thoughts she learned from church part of her said they've got to get married before the baby came or the baby would be illegitimate. Madelyn didn't want this baby to hear that all her life.

Madelyn thought well maybe Mother would agree to the marriage after all this time of being away from her so she called her Mother and asked her to sign papers. She still wouldn't get off her high horse even if it meant that this baby would be illegitimate. (Beliefs and conditioning.) They did the next best thing they went to the next state, Michigan. The law there was a person had to be 18 to get married without parent's signature... so they went and were married.

They had a couple of friends stand up for them. They went before the Justice of the Peace and when they were getting married a guy came in to buy license plates. She got married in her coat but they got married.

Jerry went out midnight shift and the drinking went on. The fighting went on.

She was hoping to have the baby on New Year's Day since she was due on December 15th 1969. She was way over that due date. According to the Doctors she was due then, but her calculations said she was due on January 19th 1970.

Camila came on January 13, 1970. Mother after all came to stay to teach Madelyn how to take care of a baby. Mother was ok then. She taught her what she knows best how to take care of a new born baby after all she had 8 children.

I guess she wanted to be a part of Camila's life even if it meant having Jerry as her son-in-law.

Camila was 6 pounds. She was beautiful. Born with a tan. Madelyn spoiled her rotten so much so that she couldn't put her down, she'd cry.

Camila wouldn't go to anyone. Madelyn took a job and made more money than Jerry but Camila cried the whole time she was gone and she have couldn't have that. So she quit to take care of Camila.

It didn't matter that they had a baby together Jerry still drank still missed work and they could hardly make ends meet. Life was worse than it was before. Madelyn was lonely. She didn't have any friends or anyone to talk to about her situation. Finally an offer came that they didn't resist.

Jerry got an offer to move back to their home town to have a job in the coal mine. Her sister's husband was a boss in the mines so he offered to help get Jerry a job.

CHAPTER 11
Moving Back

They moved back to their home town of Clark. They lived with her Sister until Jerry got the job and they saved a few pay checks and finally moved out on their own again.

Meanwhile the drinking continued. In Hamilton and in Clark it didn't matter, there was always alcohol no matter where they moved to.

Jamestown was the old stomping grounds for her husband. He stayed out all night. He had the same three shifts as before and he never worked midnights and hated day shifts. He did alright on afternoon.

One night that he didn't come home something told her to go find him so she packed up Camila and off she went to Jamestown. It so happened she passed a friend's house just in time to see Jerry drop off his old girlfriend. Madelyn suspicioned him of seeing this girl. There it was right in my face he was cheating. She couldn't help herself screaming at him that she caught him. He came home ...they fought.

She was broken. It was her fault. She didn't give him enough sex or she didn't cater to him enough but it was her fault. He even said as much!

She thought about life without him but the same fear came to haunt her. What would she do how would she make a living how could she live without him? Was she in love with this man? She forgave him.

They stayed together and she ended up pregnant. They decided to buy a house where else but Jamestown.

Madelyn and her brother-in-law moved furniture down about 15 steps her being pregnant. Jerry in the meanwhile had gotten hurt in a mine accident where the top fell in on him and broke his ankle and damaged his back.

He couldn't help move furniture he couldn't help do anything with the exception of the twelve ounce curls (beer).

She was 20 years old at the time. They immediately became friends with the neighbors. Melvin and Nancy. Melvin was a creepy old guy. He eventually tried to molest her. He was a feely touchy type of guy. Oww! Bug off old man but she didn't know how to keep him from trying to touch her all the time. She tried to tell Jerry but he just brushed it off.

Everyone in that little neighborhood hated her. The neighbor behind them was a State Highway patrolman and his wife was a niece of Melvin and Roses'. Madelyn was young. She was a hard worker. She kept the grass cut and worked outside and cleaned all the time. That's what her Mother taught her. That was her belief. Work hard. She didn't have a vacuum sweeper so she asked Rose to borrow hers and of course Rose let her. They Rose and Melvin were raising Rose's sister's daughter Jessica. Rose's sister died of cancer.

One time she remembers returning the vacuum while Melvin was home. Hoping she wouldn't run into him she took the vacuum in quietly then heard footsteps she started running for the door and the footsteps caught up to her. It was Jessica. She was relieved but then she had to explain why she was running towards the door. She couldn't tell her that her Uncle was a pervert.

As Jessica got older one day moved out of their house and back in with her Father. Madelyn never knew why it happened so suddenly.

Melvin and Nancy had sons and those son's had wives. Oh boy. The sons were flirty. They'd come to talk with Madelyn while she was outside cutting the grass. That all became a bad situation. The wives hated her. They all accused her of trying to steal their man even the neighbor behind her accused her husband of flirting with Madelyn. She tried to keep too herself.

Nancy was a kindergarten school teacher and she asked if she could take Camila to start kindergarten with her. She loved Camila. So of course she trusted her and said yes. It worked out quit well.

Melvin and Nancy invited Jerry and Madelyn out to their cabin at the lake. Everyone drank out there so Jerry was in his height of glory. Madelyn of course was a loner because none of the wives liked her so she was the one in the corner with no one to talk to. Of course with the low- self-esteem she knew she didn't fit in. They drank she didn't. She felt fat they weren't. She was only tolerated because of her husband and they all loved Camila.

Melvin was a real creep. Madelyn was miscarrying the baby she was pregnant with and Jerry and she were at the lake She needed to get back home to see a Doctor. Melvin was the only one available to take her. Jerry was drunk. Melvin on the way back tried to talk her into having sex with him grabbing at her and trying to feel her and the only reason she was saved was the fact that she was bleeding and miscarrying the baby. No one would believe her if she told on him anyway. No one believed her before when the neighbor guy attacked her so who'd believe her now especially when they all thought she was sleeping with their husbands.

She had already miscarried the baby at the lake in an outside toilet. She was 6 weeks pregnant. She just needed to see a doctor.

She went to the hospital without Jerry and had a D and C done. Camila stayed with Madelyn's sister in law, Lisa. Madelyn loved Lisa. She was a great lady but badly abused by her husband.

Not long after the miscarriage Madelyn became pregnant again. The pregnancy was too soon after the D and C. Madelyn wasn't healed enough inside to carry another baby so soon.

In between Jerry being drunk and Madelyn in an out of the hospital with this bleeding then she ended up staying at her Mother's for a while she was on complete bedrest. They took care of Camila while Jerry worked and he didn't come there because he was drunk most nights.

Every night she cried because she listened to Mother and Father talk about Jerry what a bad father and husband he was and Father saying that she was going to be this lonely old lady walking down the street with all these children and no father. That something bad had to happen before Jerry straightened up and became the husband and father he was supposed to be.

Finally, she got to go home. Complete bedrest though. She was watching TV and the sun came shining through the window onto the TV screen and she couldn't see a thing. She had stopped bleeding and she decided to move the TV on the stand so the sun wouldn't shine on it... She did.

That night she started bleeding so hard that she had to be taken to the hospital.

She was told that the bleeding couldn't be stopped that she would have this baby and Madelyn was only five and half month pregnant. Her baby was born that night a still born little girl. As Madelyn was told she was perfect in every visual way. The placenta was pulling away from the baby and she would have had multiple problems if she would have lived.

Madelyn thought the baby must've had a lot of Karma and gave her short life in order to rid herself of the Karma to have a perfect life in her next human form. Life is never ending in Madelyn's belief. She'd rather believe that then think that she would go to purgatory because she wasn't baptized.

It was three years after she lost those two babies before she had another baby and this baby was planned. There was a lot going on in those 3 years. A lot of fighting and drinking and cheating. It wasn't only Jerry it was Madelyn to. He'd cheat and would leave her, so she dated for revenge. Just looking for someone to love her. Jerry would then become the husband and father he was supposed to be because he was jealous.

She just continued forgiving Jerry when he'd come back after his affairs. She guesses in a way that she still loved Jerry and would've like to stay with him if only he could stop drinking and be a husband and father.

She just knew she wouldn't be able to make it on her own so she stuck it out with Jerry.

CHAPTER 12
Miserable Life

The roof leaked the neighbors hated her. Her husband cheated on her. Her life wasn't any better than when she lived with her Mother. It was a different kind of abuse though it was all verbal and disrespectful. It was hoping for a life that for some reason she felt that she didn't deserve.

She did have a good friend who helped her through the rough times. She was her best friend at that time. They spent a lot of time together. Gloria warned her of the times that Jerry was three miles away with another women.

She had another friend Jerry's sister. She was like a Mom to her. She loved Camila and baby sat a lot. She had six kids and a very abusive husband one who beat her. All of the kids were afraid of him. He just didn't care when he was angry who he hit first. He'd marched those boys in the house and just whacked one of them didn't care which one just started hitting them.

Things would get better than they'd get worse again. Madelyn had a babysitter come to the house and Jerry started having an affair with her. Madelyn had not a clue for a while until he started brushing his teeth oftener. He'd get all cleaned up and go out.

He finally told her one day that he was seeing someone else. He wanted a divorce. She didn't know who she could be but it didn't surprise her when he told her he was having another affair. It was a surprise when she found out he was having an affair with the baby sitter she was barely sixteen.

Madelyn called the babysitter and told her if she didn't quit seeing her husband who was much older than the babysitter she'd have a talk with her parents. So the affair ended.

They tried to make a go of it again and she forgave him again. They planned another baby. She didn't know what she was thinking at that time. Probably that with another child he'd be different and stop drinking. She knew nothing about addiction. She got pregnant and they were blessed with another daughter. Christina another 6 pounds baby girl… She had light colored hair. It was kind of reddish blonde. She was beautiful. She looked like Camila only different color hair. Her kids were the joy in her life and kept her happy for a while but it was very overwhelming when both the kids were sick with ear aches and Jerry was out drinking and Madelyn was alone without a car and lived way out in the country. Jerry didn't change at all. His addiction was stronger than any member of the family.

The kids were the only little people who kept her going, that unconditional love. She had to do what she had to do in order to take care of her children and if that meant staying with Jerry then so be it.

Madelyn and Jerry always had problems with their furnace in that house. Madelyn had to go to the basement and replace a screw in fuse. It blew from the wet and dampness in the almost basement that was there. She'd walk this narrow board to the fuse box. It was a kind of bridge across all the water that was in the basement and unscrew the old fuse and replace it. It's a wonder she didn't get electrocuted.

They had crick rats too. They came in the house through the various holes in the floor and their almost basement under the house. They were huge. Our friends Gloria and Tim and their daughter would come over and a rat was in their hall wall. Their daughter was saying look daddy a cat. It was a huge rat that was disoriented from the poison they had put down to kill them. Tim grabbed a hammer and killed it. They used to fall out from underneath the cupboards when Madelyn stood in the kitchen cooking. They'd fall onto her feet. She'd grab the broom and sweep them outside to freeze in the middle of winter.

Jerry even tried to make her feel guilty about sweeping the rat outside to freeze.

The furnace went out one night late so she'd called her parents to come get them. That night the house caught on fire. It was the fuse box under the house. Jerry was at work and her Siamese cat was still in the house. When the phone rang and she was told by Mother that their house was burning down they didn't go to the house they just stayed in bed. Mother and Father weren't interested in getting up and going to see it. She was in her Mother's house and wouldn't even ask to go. Mother still had emotional control over Madelyn's decision making. She just laid in bed and cried. She'd lost so much and nobody even cared and her poor cat... still in house.

The next day she went to her burned house and cried. She thought she'd lost her cat in the fire but somehow Slippers safely made it out. She was scared but she came to Madelyn but she had no- where to take her. Her friends Gloria and Tim said they'd keep Slippers and if they needed a place to stay they could come live with them until Madelyn and Jerry figured out what they were going to do.

They had no- where to go. Mother offered but she just couldn't put her kids through that abusive situation. She thought she'd treat them the same way she treated Madelyn growing up.

They took Gloria and Tim up on their offer.

CHAPTER 13
Making Decisions

Iit was a hell of a winter. It snowed so hard and deep and the pump house pump froze and they had no running water. They had a fire place that the heat went up the chimney not into the house. They broke the ice on the crick that run past the country home so they could clean the house and bath. They took all the dirty clothes to Madelyn's Mother's. They washed clothes in a wringer washer but thank goodness she had a dryer. No hanging the clothes in the basement like when she was a kid in the winter.

Madelyn was thankful that her Mother helped them at that time. As she recalls her Mother didn't make her feel like crap. They got along well but she made her friend feel like crap so Gloria wouldn't go to Mother's to wash clothes.

Life there was rough with no running water and having to carry it from the (crick) as we called it, was a chore. It was so cold that you could see your breath in the mornings when you woke up and if you took anything to drink with you to bed it was frozen by morning. They managed though.

They had insurance on their house that burned down. They bought a used mobile home to put back on the property with the insurance money. They had to wait until winter was over though and it seemed forever because of the cold and snow and then the spring time mud held them up.

It was an interesting time in her life. Madelyn was introduced to pot. You know marijuana.

Actually, the first time she was held down and smoke blown in her face. Everyone there smoked pot except her. She was told it lead to harder drugs and Jerry smoked pot and when Madelyn got into a fight with him he just laughed at her which mad her angry. He'd try to grow pot at the other house before it burned and when she was angry at him she took it and threw it over the porch.

To her it was the root of all evil. Well, that didn't last long. She couldn't beat them so she joined them. She actually liked it. She never laughed so hard in her entire life. She was serious about everything and it felt good to let loose and just laugh about stupid stuff. So relaxing.

The two families together had people stop all the time getting them high. Then they started playing Euchre, a card game they all loved. They had loads of friends come to play and they'd get high and eat. They were on teams and played until early morning.

Jerry of course missed a lot of work and stayed out half the night drinking and came home just to pick a fight with Madelyn so he could go back out again. Madelyn thought he was jealous because her whole attention wasn't on him. She was always having fun now and he didn't like that very much. She wasn't alone and became braver to say what she had to say to him. She was tired of his crap. He was losing control over her and he didn't like it. Her world became a constant upheaval because he was unhappy with her and her new friendships.

The straw that broke the camels back finally came when Jerry came in the house one evening drunk and blamed her for the car getting stuck in three foot of snow and he couldn't get it out. He was driving the car not her so why was it her fault? He demanded her to go push him out, the good little wife that she was went out and pushed the car while he sat inside telling her what a whore she was and how she screwed everyone in Jamestown, and she was a good for nothing wife and no one would ever want or love her. OH MY GOD!! She had had enough she turned into her Mother. She reached in the car window and grabbed him by his hair and just started pounding him wherever she could. She was out of control with anger and tears and so much hurt. How could anyone who loved her say those horrible things?

Jerry got out of the car and as usual said" I don't have to take this" and started walking.

She got that car out. She went into the house and used the ashes from the fireplace and drove that car out. By then he was gone and that's when she made the decision to divorce him again only this time she meant it. She was done with his lazy ass and blaming her for everything that went wrong. It was time for her to move on. Things happen for a reason. She believed that living there and finding out there was another kind of life outside of being stuck out in the country with a husband that the only thing he cared about was feeding his addiction. She'd find a better life than living with him.

But Oh no. She missed a period. NO...NO...NO this can't be happening. She didn't want another baby not to him. It was her fault she was getting high and thought she had taken her pills but when she looked she had missed like 4 days and it was too late she was pregnant.

She didn't care though. Abortion looked pretty good at that moment even though she didn't believe in it, at all. She made the appointment to see the Doctor and started looking at all those baby magazines she made up her mind that no she couldn't have an abortion she wanted this baby maybe she'd have a boy this time. But... she was still determined to get a divorce... pregnant or not.

CHAPTER 14
Moving On Their Own

The mobile home finally was put on the property. They moved in but she was determined to go through with the divorce. She couldn't live with this verbally abusive man any longer than necessary.

Jerry still missed work he still did the same abusive verbal assaults and that baby didn't belong to him. That just made it that much easier to divorce his ass. She had to wait though until the income tax check came in.

The check finally came and she put it under lock and key. She doesn't know why she waited she said she believed she was waiting on the baby to be born. Waiting on a miracle to happen? She knew better though Jerry would never change. He loved his alcohol too much.

In the mean time she went out with her friend Gloria and ran into her ex -boyfriend from high school.

They enjoyed each other's company. They went to a dance and watched everyone else dance and they talked about her husband and his wife. Yes, he was married.... and her to ... Madelyn was pregnant and guess what Veronica was too. Six Weeks!!

So, our date was just catching up.

Eddie was a drug person. He used to come to Madelyn's house while she was just married to Jerry by about three years and would bring pot and some sort of pills and asked if Madelyn wanted any. She promptly showed him the door. No drugs. That's when it was drilled into her head that pot drove a person to heavier drugs and he definitely had harder drugs.

He showed up every year on her birthday to wish her a happy birthday and tell her he still loved her. She just ignored him because she was in love with Jerry.

Well, the time came when she no longer loved Jerry. He was verbally abusive and he just didn't deserve her forgiveness anymore.

Eddie had a talent and he had a good job and he loved what he did. One problem …actually two.

He was married and was going to have a baby. That ended that idea. Madelyn wasn't about to break up anyone's marriage especially when Veronica was pregnant with her first child and Eddie's first child.

It didn't take long though until he was calling her and asking her out. She couldn't resist she had to find love again and Jerry was just not going to work and did nothing but drink and go out with his friends.

She cheated and kept on cheating. Jerry guessed but she wouldn't admit she was. Jerry didn't trust her to go to the store by herself. He sent a friend with her so she wouldn't try to see Eddie.

Jerry slept in the living room and she slept in the bedroom. He paid more attention to her then, then he ever did before. She just didn't care anymore. It was too late.

Jerry got hurt again in the mine and he was off work for about three months. Oh my goodness she hated it. He had his friends moving in with them. One friend moved in and his wife thought he and Madelyn were sleeping together. . Jerry had another young guy move in "Butch" he was like a son to her. Ten years younger. He was great. He helped her with the kids helped with the grocery shopping. Cleaned up with dishes. She needed all the help she could get. Jerry didn't help. He was too busy drinking.

Finally, one night alone and one week before the baby was due Madelyn went into labor. She woke up in the middle of the night and realized she was in labor and knew what the pain was and went back to sleep until 7am. She called Gloria she came over and then Madelyn woke Jerry.

The biggest surprise happened. As they was walking across the parking lot it was snowing lightly. It was November 12th 1977, and a voice from above yelled out and said "Hey are you coming to the hospital to have the baby, we've been here since about 4 am". I looked up and it was Eddie. Veronica had gone into labor to. She was due November 1st and Madelyn wasn't due until the 19th. What were the chances they'd go into labor the same day and be at the same hospital together? Thank goodness they weren't in the same room. There are no coincidences. Hummm!

Ok, Universe what was this all about?

Madelyn went straight into the labor room opposite Veronica and not long after, Madelyn was taken to delivery. When she went through those doors she thought to herself "I hate this part. It hurts so bad...

She wasn't in there long. This was her forth birth and she knew the drill. Candi was born a little after 9am... 6 pounds. Long dark hair beautiful just like Madelyn's other two girls. No boy but she didn't care Candi was healthy.

Poor Veronica was in labor for another 10 hours before she had Erin.

After Candi's birth, Eddie came into Madelyn's room and asked her to not have a tubal ligation so they could have a baby together.

That was out of the question. She didn't want another baby. Three was enough and she didn't know how she was going to support the three she already had. She was getting a divorce.

CHAPTER 15
Home with Baby

Madelyn didn't hear from Eddie for a while. She knew that having a son changed his mind about Eddie and Madelyn getting together. He wanted to stay with Veronica so he could raise his son with her and that was ok. Madelyn understood. She deserved to be left alone. Madelyn was still determined to divorce Jerry. She didn't want her kids to grow up with an alcoholic father.

Eddie called after a while and wanted to see her again. He wanted her to move out away from Jerry and get a place of her own and he was going to help her. It took him until spring to call again and Madelyn was more than ready. She had the baby blues. She cried all the time. She couldn't keep up with the kids and the house work. Jerry brought his friends in and cooked and left the mess for her to clean. She was so over whelmed by everything.

Finally the time came. Eddie found a place, remodeled it and she was on her way out the door. Jerry knew then that she was moving out. He said if she'd leave he'd never have anything to do with the kids and wouldn't pay child support. He stood true to his word for the first time in their life together.

The day she moved was a stressful day. Jerry was supposed to stay away while the furniture was being moved out but he came home drunk and with every piece of furniture moved he had something to say. Everything was about sex. We made Candi on that bed. We had sex on that couch. She just wanted him to go away. She didn't know where her loyalties were supposed to be. She was moving out but she felt sorry for him. Her head was mixed up. Why was she so conflicted she wondered?

She left the mobile home for him to live in and left the electric and water on for him. Out of GUILT! He abused her kindness and never paid the electric or the water bills. He had a bunch of puppies born to a dog that he and his friends just left to starve to death in the yard and the grass was never cut. When he and his friends left and Madelyn went to the mobile home after she had the water and electric turned off. What a disaster she walked into. They left a freezer full of deer meat unthawed and the blood dripped onto the kitchen carpet and the toilet was full of shit, not flushed. The place was a disaster.

She cleaned it all up and locked everything up and put it up for sale. Her sister Elaine and her then husband bought it. They moved it off the lot and sold it. The property was put up for sale and the creepy old man neighbor wanted to buy it so she sold it to him for some ridiculous high price and he bought it.

She said once before she didn't know where her loyalties lay at the time. She was married to Jerry and living with Eddie. She collected the money for both the mobile home and the property after she sold them and kept the money. Jerry bugged her to death about giving him half the money. The only thing that was in her mind was that ass didn't pay the electric bill and the water and they left that mess for her to clean and he didn't give her one dime of child support and he wanted half the money...Ha.... fat chance of that happening. She knew then where her loyalties lie with her and the kids. On the other hand Eddie was a shyster to, when it came to money, he wanted her to buy a boat for their pleasure of course. What he really meant was for him and his friends' pleasure. At the time her self-esteem was so low she'd do anything for them to spend time together something different then what she'd been through with Jerry.

CHAPTER 16

Eddie

M adelyn felt a relief moving out of that mobile home away from her husband who tormented her with lies and drinking and cheating. She didn't know how she was going to make it but was determined.

Little did she know that her life would become another mess, Eddie was never alone or never home. They had someone at the house at all times it seemed. No alone time with him and when they didn't have company they had his son and her three children. She had twins. Eric and Candi the same age. Five months old. Eddie's and Veronica's son and Madelyn's and Jerry's 3 girls.

She spent time with Eddie when he had Erin. When they had company they were not together. He wanted to spend time with his friends and he told her so. "He said I see you every day when my friends come I want to spend time with them not you".

Eddie was a partier. He loved to smoke pot and drink beer and whatever other drug she didn't know about. He loved to sneak off and get away from her. She was in love though she was ready to get married and she went places with him while the kids were in school. Work related places.

She thought he was so much in love with her he wanted to do the same thing. Boy was she wrong.

He wanted her to get divorced right away and not to take forever and she obliged. Madelyn and Jerry got a dissolution of marriage and she was granted $400 a month child support which she never seen a dime of until she took him back to court and they awarded her fifty dollars a month because he had no income. He quit the coal mine and only got a government check and Madelyn got half. He stood to his promise. He'd never get a job until Candi turned eighteen. Eddie took a year to get divorced. Then Madelyn was ready to get married again and when she asked him about it he said" I guess we could... you and the kids would be a good tax deduction".

What? Wait a minute you just want to get married because of a tax write off? She told him to forget it.

She was determined not to think about marriage until he was sincere. It never happened not for a few more years. When he was finally ready he just wanted a big party as usual.

He didn't want to be with her. He was in love with the fact that they were an item at one time and he had to have her because once Madelyn was in his life again he took her for granted.

She let it all happen. She had no self- esteem. She felt she was stuck again. It was a richer life and they had more money all the time but she had no sex life at all. That got to her. She had one marriage where Jerry couldn't get enough sex so he cheated on her all the time and now Eddie didn't like sex. He wasn't interested in sex... with her. He said he didn't have the desire. HUUMMMMM!!!!

They did things together. Got drunk. Went to the bars and spent time with his friends. She was alone again. Only this time he was there but not in mind and heart.

She was always angry because he didn't pay any attention to her. They got into fights or rather she got into fights. He had no interest so she drew interest... She started to act like Mother. She threw things and broke them and he'd say now what did you do that for we just have to buy a new one. She stopped throwing things. It didn't work anyway. He just didn't care.

They'd have parties and invite all his friends and his ex-wife. She was a part of his old friendship so she had to come. They'd all sit around together and Madelyn of course was paranoid and think they were talking about her. She'd get drunk and would go to bed. She was a light weight drinker ...just a few and she'd had enough and she'd have to find a place to crash.

That was a problem with Eddie too, why did Madelyn get drunk so fast? Why did she get so upset because his ex -wife was there at their house? Veronica would go on vacation with them she was part of his friend network. She would go to the parks with them... Madelyn was jealous. He paid more attention to his ex then he did her.

He said it was because of Erin. Eddie didn't pay child support so he invited Victoria to all their events so Erin would be allowed to come.

Veronica was an ever present in just about everything they did. If it was in other circumstances then Madelyn could have become her friend.

This very day so many tears later Madelyn ask Veronica for forgiveness because Eddie was married to her when Madelyn and Eddie got together and Veronica didn't want any kids but Eddie talked her into having Erin and then he left her for Madelyn. Madelyn felt she was in a desperate situation at the time and she thought that Eddie and she were supposed to be together so she took advantage of the situation to get herself out of a relationship that didn't work for her anymore.

Bad Karma got her. She was in a relationship that was abusive in another way and she didn't understand that at the time.

Madelyn rolled with the punches. At times things were good she almost fell in love again a few times when he paid attention to her but that alcoholic drug abuser showed his ugly head and she was back being confused about the relationship they had.

There were a few friends that he had that Madelyn could not stand. This couple were both alcoholics and when they came to their parties they fought like cats and dogs. She was an abuser and he was too. She hit him and screamed and he screamed back at her both in their drunken tyrants at whoever was in their way. Madelyn hated to see them come and when they brought their boys. Oh my Gosh Madelyn couldn't wait until they left. They gave their children beer and the boys threw up on the furniture.

After three years of living together and buying a house he decided they should get married. He seemed sincere but she thought it was just to have a party. It was a big one too... Of course they invited his ex-wife so that Erin could be in the wedding.

She felt different then. She was in love and he seemed to be to... for about a week.

As their lives progressed so did the drinking and drugs.

CHAPTER 17
Their Business

E ddie's office was in our kitchen… His employee's would come
and she'd make pots and pots of coffee. They'd smoke pot and
cigarettes and she even made lunches and Eddie gave them money for
gas so they could go to the job sight.

Madelyn would be running around getting her kids ready for
school. They'd eat breakfast in the living room in all that smoke. She
smoked to though and she got high with them. She was also addicted
to getting high. Then she'd walk her youngest to school.

When she came back from taking her youngest to school they
would all be gone. She'd proceed to her duties as a mother and wife.
Wash clothes and clean the kitchen up and plant flowers cut the grass
and trim the hedges clean the cars.

She started exercise classes with her best friend Clare. They spent a
lot of time together through the years. Usually exercise classes and just
sitting around talking about her life and Madelyn's. They were besties
who she could talk to about anything.

In the evenings Madelyn would cook dinner and wait on her
husband to come home. He'd be there with his friends with a 12 pack
of beer. If he didn't come home he'd be at a local bar drinking with
his friends and supper would be cold and she'd be frustrated with him

and angry. When he did make it home he'd be drunk and sometimes he'd eat but a lot of time he just got on the couch and went to sleep. Friday's were the worst. He came home and Madelyn was the accountant for his company and would do the payroll for everyone and the deposits at the bank. The whole crew would be there at their house. Collecting their paychecks and getting drunk and high. Then they'd have company come along and they'd be that couple that she didn't like. Both were drunks and his wife was one of those people who liked to hang on all the guys even Madelyn's daughter's boyfriend who was 18. Carol felt him on his butt and Camila hated that. Camila was only 14. Madelyn hated it to. She felt that this women should have more control over herself than to flirt with a young girl's boyfriend. Madelyn felt disrespected in her own home and to avoid a confrontation with her husband and this women she just kept her mouth shut. It was always company and always people she didn't want coming to her house. It carried on into the wee hours of the morning sometimes... She became unsociable and usually watched TV or... tried to watch TV. The noise was so loud from the company and her husband got so drunk he thought it was ok to turn up the stereo so loud that she couldn't hear the TV.

CHAPTER 18
Sister Gatherings

M adelyn would go every once in-a-while with her sisters. They'd meet up somewhere at one of the sisters houses or rent a cabin somewhere and she'd go away for the weekend with them. Joy was a shaman from the Indian Tribe. She taught them about the Indians and how they lived. There were so many things she leaned from her sister and she was happy to be with the sisters and as they related to how much they were a like for being apart for many years.

Madelyn thought it was a bitter sweet vacation. She thought she was the black sheep in the family. Madelyn smoked cigarettes and pot and did some other drugs and did some drinking but they didn't know that. {About the drugs}. In her mind she felt guilty and wasn't good enough. Any sort of advice or criticism she took to heart and thought she was being picked on, just like being at home with Mother. She cried every time she left the sister's. She felt they disrespected her and looked down on her as a black sheep would feel in the situation she was in. She wasn't good enough for them. I think Sister Elaine and Sister Margret felt the same way Madelyn did. Elaine and she talked about the younger sisters. They would criticize one of the older ones at ever gathering. One of the three would cry. Madelyn thought about it as she became older that the younger sisters were just giving advice and the older ones took it as criticism. The older ones were the three who put up with Mother's anger.

Madelyn felt that she was the one being picked on in between learning about how to live a better life. She was being taught how to love herself unconditionally. She thought that was crazy. Madelyn was conditioned to give to others and be satisfied with what she had. That a rich person wouldn't go to heaven. The man was always who a women should be subservient to. Not to be selfish and think of herself. Her kids were first in Madelyn's life. She loved them unconditionally.

According to her Mother-in-law, her husband and her Mother Madelyn was the worst mother in the world. At least that is how she felt. Looking back she knows that her self -esteem was at a mindset that she wasn't good enough for anyone not even herself. She was totally brain washed by her own mind.

She was raising her children wrong. She was easy... She knew that... in her mind she could hear her Mother yell at her that she going to amount to nothing and Madelyn didn't want her children to feel the pain she felt... so they didn't get punished, they did, but not as harsh as Madelyn remembers the punishments that were so unnecessary and painfully degrading that she received.. She thought it was easier to do it herself then to listen to them argue and cry over things like house work. Instead she took their lesson away from them not knowing that that is what she was doing. She was battered and bruised from her childhood experiences.

She was shamed for letting the children get away with not doing housework by her husband and by her own inflicted pain. She was so low and so depressed most of those years and had had a bad image of herself and she believed when someone tried to give her advice she thought they were picking on her and criticizing her for how she raised her children.

Her sister had not a problem telling her she shouldn't give into them that they should be punished. She shouldn't help them financially or help them get out of trouble. They needed to learn from their own mistakes. She agreed later in her life once she understood it was her own self sabotaging reacting to her childhood experiences. They needed to suffer the consequences of their own doings. She never made them do too much house work because she did so much as a child that she wasn't going to make them suffer like she did but unknowing she was still the one who suffered. They needed to know responsibility and she took that away from them.

Madelyn's husband on the other hand wanted to punish them when he was drunk. She did not let that happen. Madelyn was a mouse who took abuse from everyone. But she would not let anyone hurt her children. She felt she deserved what was handed to her but not her children.

After a few years of the sister gathering Madelyn's husband said that she had changed. She wasn't the wife he married. Madelyn had started to love herself and was starting to learn that what was happening to her was abuse in another form.

CHAPTER 19
Motor Cycle Group

Eddie decided he wanted to join a motorcycle group. As if she didn't have enough problems... now he wanted to be in a biker group. Eddie attended the meetings every Sunday and one day he called her and wanted her to be proud of him because he decided he wanted to be in this group and they named him the Road Captain and he was going to prospect for the group, for parties, for his fellow bikers. Madelyn was "not" proud of him. She thought to herself "when are you going to grow up and be a husband and father that you promised when they got together".

He bought a bike in a basket. "LITERALLY" in a basket. His fellow bikers helped build his bike. They'd go to the biker bashes and she'd be alone most of the time. She had nothing in common with these people and she'd get a little tipsy and speak out against them. Eddie would grab me from behind because he knew she was drunk and he'd put his hand over her mouth so no one could hear her say what chauvinist bikers were. He'd warn her that there would be trouble and she needed to keep her mouth shut. He had control over her. She wanted this man to love her.

She stayed thin. She exercised. She was a model wife. She was most of the time seen but not heard. She put up with all the stuff he did. She left her daughter to babysit her children when they needed her at home. She needed that love. No one loved her. She wanted her Mother to hold her and say it's going to be alright or her Father who was never emotionally available. She just needed someone to love her.

There were plenty of guys who wanted to love her but it was only for sex not love. Eddie's friends were the worst.

Madelyn was young, long hair to her waist. She was nice to everyone and done as she was told. She was good to Eddie's Mother. She did what she asked but behind Madelyn's back his Mother talked about her and her girls. She said Madelyn run a whore house letting guy's stay at the house with her daughter's. They were the girl's boyfriends not random guy's like she made it sound to her relatives who either liked to make Madelyn miserable by telling her what his Mother was saying or just back stabbers who liked to cause trouble.

She put up with drunks in and out of her house. Ones that tried to put the make on her and in the middle of the night she'd have people walk into her house with cocaine to divide up on her kitchen table. She'd get out of bed and see that happening and she was fit to be tied. Eddie knew how she felt about drugs but yet he allowed it to happen even when her girls were upstairs in bed.

She wanted to leave him or divorce him but fear kept her locked up in that relationship. After years of putting up with his drunken behavior of disrespecting her and the children and their home, and learning through her sisters that what she was putting up with was not in her best interest. She started to rebel. She started to fight the situation she spoke out but Eddie didn't care. He just listened and ignored her. He never fought back until he started harder drugs and drinking heavier... hard liquor and cocaine.

He came home from work one day and told Madelyn that her oldest daughter was seeing a black man. His fellow biker friend told him he saw Camila walking with a black guy and she should know that the "bikers" would not put up with one of their members' daughters being with black individuals.

Madelyn asked Camila about this black young man and she said it was a guy she went to school with and they had a summer job with the school cleaning the school and they walked home together. She told Eddie and he didn't believe me he believed his Biker brothers.

Well now, you know you don't pick on her kids. She didn't care what the Bikers think. Everything that hurt her in the past came out in that argument and the shit hit the fan as they say. Just an excuse for him to go out and get drunk with his friends. Later all was forgiven but he still didn't believe her though.

They got a new friends in their life, a lawyer Joe and his wife Lizza. How they met was, they crashed their wedding. Eddie, Madelyn Lizza and Joe became very good friends. They went everywhere together.

They planned vacations in the Bahamas and in Mexico. They went to the bikers bashes. Madelyn finally had another friends that both Eddie and Madelyn related to without Eddie's ex-wife in the group.... Madelyn never imagined getting a good friend outside the ones she already had but with this friend the husbands were friends too.

Lizza worked for her husband as a secretary. She'd call Madelyn and asked her to come out to the house or come with her to lunch. Madelyn loved having a new friend.

Madelyn's, other best friend was Clare. Clare and Madelyn were members of an exercise club. They'd go exercise then visit for the day sometimes they would go eat lunch then she'd go home and Madelyn would then start dinner.

Their lives took different paths when Clare got pregnant with her last child. Madelyn was over that period of her life. So, Clare had a baby and Madelyn got a job, "cleaning". What else was she good at? As far as Madelyn was concerned she couldn't do anything else. She was living with the belief that she couldn't do anything. She didn't have an education.

She did keep the books for her husband's company but she didn't think she was doing a very good job. Her husband didn't want to pay Madelyn because the more money they made the more taxes they'd have to pay.

Madelyn even wondered why her new friend liked her so much. Why was she calling her and wanting to be her friend. Madelyn didn't believe enough in herself to think she could make another good friend who wanted to spend time with her.

Madelyn was a sort of a home body. She stayed home a lot. She was a little obsessive compulsive when it came to keeping the house clean and she tried to stay close by just in case her kids might need her even though they were old enough to take care of themselves. She had this anxiety that if she wasn't there and something would happen she'd feel really guilty. She'd then be a bad Mother in other people's eyes. She worried what people thought about her.

The drugs became a priority in this stage of her life not for her but for her husband. Cocaine was introduced into their world. She used the same as they did but soon she decided it wasn't the kind of life she wanted to live. What if she became addicted then who would take care of her kids. Nobody could love them the way she did. She just wanted family life not the drugs not the drinking. She wondered if Eddie would ever become that family man he always said he wanted.

CHAPTER 20

Incorporation

E ddie's business became successful and he decided he would incorporate his business. Their lawyer told them it would a new ball game of paying a lot of money out, paying disability insurance, paying quarterly taxes, federal taxes, and hiring a tax accountant. Eddie thought he'd make it though so he incorporated.

Once the business got off to a good start Eddie's son had to have an operation. He was 15. As a child Erin was born with a pinched artery coming out of his heart. At five years old he went to Children's hospital and the Doctors attached an artery coming out from his arm and attached it to his artery coming out of his heart. That artery flowed blood to the lower part of his body.

At the age of ten still having issues with his blood pressure the Doctors sent him to Children's Hospital again to do an angioplasty. When the Doctors did the angioplasty they couldn't open the artery. The artery attached with the last surgery didn't grow any bigger and it curved in a downward position and they were afraid the artery would break. The Doctors decided then that they would wait until puberty when he stopped growing as fast.

At fifteen Erin again was taken to the Children's Hospital and again was taken into surgery and the Doctor went through the ribs and tried to fix the artery. The Doctor thought it would be a quick fix and didn't put him on a by-pass machine. A machine that would keep the blood flowing through his body while he repaired his heart artery. He worked on Erin and decided that he didn't like the fix and decided to do it over. In the midst of the surgery Erin's artery was too weak and blew open and his blood was cut off from his heart and the rest of his body. The surgery went on as quickly as it could be done while the nurse that was keeping the family updated told them that the Doctor was working to keep Erin alive. Details were few and far between.

Erin made it through the surgery but now there was a waiting game was he going to wake up or was he going to be in a coma. Also there was the possibility of him being a paraplegic or a quadriplegic.

Erin woke up and the Doctors told him he was going to be paralyzed from the waist down. He tried to get out of the bed that day. It was so sad to watch him struggle.

The next day was a blur. Madelyn knew she had to give Eddie and Veronica her blessing. Their son needed them and Madelyn knew that her feelings of them being together was not important at that time.

Erin then ended up with a staff- infection and the Doctors knew he had to keep the infection under control or it would go to his heart and he would die as a result.

Eddie stayed at the hospital for three months. He came home on the weekends to see how the business was doing but amongst the employee was a lot of friction and they took advantage of the situation and went home early but reported forty hours a week. The only thing that Madilyn could do was do their paychecks according to how they reported their work hours.

Madelyn wanted to comfort Eddie but he was more interested in drinking with his friends. Apparently Madelyn was not one of those friends. She was an outcast as usual.

Eventually the business went under. Taxes weren't paid. The federal government threatened to take their lively hood away and seized their bank accounts. There was no pleasing the government. They were determined to ruin Eddie and Madelyn's lives.

They tried to keep the business together and Eddie did to some extent but the government was always a threat. Madelyn was working but only made minimum wage just enough to keep food on the table. It still didn't stop the drinking though or the drugs.

CHAPTER 21

Every New Eve they would rent a Hotel room and there would be a New Year's Eve party at the hotel. Every year Madelyn ended up angry at everyone because they spent most of their time running back to the hotel room snorting cocaine. Actually, she just wanted to go home and see if her kids were ok.

The next day they'd end up at a friend's house for a few hours that next morning into the afternoon. Finally they all went home. That's when Eddie would sleep and Madelyn would take care of home chores. The kids were older now but still Madelyn worried about them and wondered what they did on New Year's Eve?

A lot of the times in the winter months Eddie wouldn't have any work but that didn't stop him from going to visit his friends and coming home drunk.

Madelyn was miserable most of the time. She cried every day. She just didn't know how to stop what was going on. To her this was not a normal way of living. She was conditioned to live a boring normal life. Like her parents did. Madelyn was afraid to have fun. She would be judged.

Camila was 15. She had a steady boyfriend but he liked to drink too and smoke pot. He left her alone a lot and she was anxious and didn't want to be tied down and wait on him to come around when he was ready. She started dating a new boy older than her, a lot older ...and she ended up getting pregnant.

Panic stricken with the pending news Madelyn had to tell her husband, she had to tell her mother. She had to let all her friends her fifteen year old daughter was pregnant. Madelyn was 34 years old and going to be a grandmother. Wasn't that really young to be a grandmother?

She was afraid to break the news to them all because of the repercussions she was going to get from Madelyn's mistake of letting Camila do what she wanted. It was Madelyn's fault. She could hear her Mother say that she wasn't a very good Mother she was naive and stupid and didn't know shit about raising kids. Madelyn believed she didn't have an example of how to raise the kids. Her Mother was abusive. Madelyn wasn't going to raise her kids like that afraid of Madelyn and couldn't come to her for support. Madelyn had to figure out how to raise them another way but she had no instructions so she did the best she could. But at that point she thought she had done a terrible job. She let her thoughts go crazy which caused anxiety. She didn't know how to stop the thoughts from coming. What if?

Well that was one of the worst news events she'd ever had to reveal. Her friends of course said "make her get an abortion". Eddie said that she had ruined her life "get an abortion". Needless to say he was very upset and had to get drunk. Camila's boyfriend was so in love with her that he said he'd raise the baby as his own. She wanted to be with this other man but Madelyn knew she'd have a miserable life with him to. His whole family were drinkers and drug abusers. The biological father would call and beg Madelyn to let him be with Camila but Madelyn always said NO.

Now she had to tell her Mother. Mother said she's nothing but a whore. She sleeps around with everyone and she's just a whore. Madelyn was so angry but still her Mother had control over Madelyn's and Madelyn said nothing to her Mother. It was like she was back there in that house again taking the abuse only this time she was insulting Madelyn's child and her own grandchild. Madelyn lost her voice. Flight or fight? Madelyn chose to flight. Out the door she'd go and walk off the pain she carried in her soul and then when no one was home she'd write it all down and read it and throw it away.

Her sister drove from Webster with her crying son all the way to tell Madelyn that she should give the baby up for adoption. It wasn't Madelyn's decision to give up the baby it was the Mother's decision. Camila had the right to say whether she wanted to give the baby up or keep the baby. Needless to say she wanted the baby. This baby was Madelyn's first grandchild how could she try to convince her daughter to give the baby up for adoption. She couldn't show how excited she was to have a first grandchild. She didn't want criticized for wanting this baby. Madelyn was glad she was taken out of the equation to have the say over the baby being adopted. Instead Madelyn decided to support her daughter in any way she could that would help in having and raising the baby.

Eddie came in drunk and told Madelyn Camila was ruining her life by having a baby that young. Camila told him that nobody loved her and she was always babysitting anyway so why not have a baby that would love her unconditionally. For her to say that, hurt Madelyn because she loved her with her heart but she didn't know how to show her physically by hugging her. Madelyn felt awkward about physically hugging her children. When she was younger her parents didn't hug her growing up. She didn't know how to show her children that kind of love. She was never taught, and to hold her children in her arms as young adults was something she didn't learn until much later in life. She didn't realize it at the time but she was doing to her children what her Mother and Father did to her when she was growing up.

That was learned behavior. Madelyn's Mother and Father hugged them at night before bed but just to get a hug for no reason that never happened.

Eddie was still the drunk. He worked every day though. They went with their new friends to dinner and Eddie became a hard liquor drinker. Beer to start out then a martini then more beer then a Martini then more beer then a shot of Jack Daniels then a little cocaine. Dinner took forever because of the drinking. Madelyn started drinking heavier also. She drank Vodka and OJ or cranberry. At the end of dinner she'd drink a coffee with Irish cream.

She always watched that she didn't get drunk. She was usually the designated driver. She wanted to go home and didn't want to stay at anyone's house. Eddie just wanted to stay and drink further into the night. She didn't stay though she always drove home.

It was nice to have someone to talk to about Eddie. She complained about him all the time to her friend. She didn't care what Lizza and her husband did because they were just as bad as Eddie and even worse than Eddie when it came to drinking but they were in it together. They vacationed together they went on date night together. They loved each other. They partied a lot. But they had a very good relationship and knew how to keep it together for each other.

Joe joined the Motor Cycle Group. Together the two couples rode motorcycles. It was fun riding. Madelyn and Eddie had a lot of parties at their house with all the bikers and other friends. It was hard to raise a family when you're a biker chick.

Madelyn's kids hated it but she just didn't know how to stop it. The children were older now and able to take care of themselves.

The parties at the clubhouse were long and at the end of the late night there were contests. Nudity was a part of the contest. That's when she went to the van. She hated to watch those girls disrespect themselves in front of a bunch of guys. Eddie tried to get her to do it "Absolutely not". She was brain washed by this man and fear drove her to stay with him but that was somethings she wouldn't do.

CHAPTER 22

Too Close for Comfort

E ddie's friend's Bruce and Carol the ones that fought at every party.
Carol was fond of feeling young guy's butt's. Bruce and Eddie
were best friends from the past who took care of Eddie after Eddie had
gotten out of the service.

Bruce became very sick and had to have a liver transplant. Bruce
and his wife drank a lot but before the liver transplant Bruce had to stop
drinking for six months before they would put him on the transplant
list. Bruce then had the liver transplant he had to stop drinking but she
didn't. He then stopped the cycle of the fighting. She wanted to... but
he just didn't fight with her anymore.

Bruce ended up getting a kidney transplant then another liver
transplant and ended up dying of lung cancer. He told Eddie before he
died that he didn't think he was going to be around long and would
Eddie take care of his wife after he was gone. Madelyn didn't like this
girl at all and she didn't like the idea of Eddie taking care of her.

Carol loved motorcycles and wanted Eddie to give her a ride.
Madelyn said absolutely not. She didn't like her at all and she seemed
to always be trying to make Madelyn jealous, and she was. Eddie paid
more attention to her than he did Madelyn. He knew how Madelyn felt
about her but yet he said it was Madelyn's problem not his.

On one occasion Eddie and Carol and other friends were all somewhere together and they ran out of beer. Eddie took her to buy beer on the back of the motor cycle and she got that ride she wanted. Madelyn found out much later when it was mentioned at a bar and Madelyn's daughter was present when the story was told.

Months later when Bruce was really sick again Carol came to their house to tell Eddie that Bruce was dying of Cancer. It was about 9 am Carol was already drinking and Eddie got more beer and they proceeded to get drunker in Eddie's office while Madelyn maintained her family life with the kids. Eddie came in the kitchen and said he was going with Carol. She was going to drop him off at a friend's body shop. Madelyn was ok with that. At 9 pm she called the shop to see where Eddie was and the bod shop owner said he left at noon with Carol. Ok. What's going on here? Madelyn couldn't stand or trust this girl and he is with her all day getting drunker.

It was all innocent of course. According to Eddie. Nothing happened.

On another occasion a few close friends and Eddie and Madelyn were going to go out to dinner one Saturday evening and Eddie wanted to visit Bruce and he'd be back to go to dinner. He took the motorcycle.

Madelyn waited and when it came time to go to dinner Eddie was a no show. She called Bruce's house and they told Madelyn that Eddie and Carol had left to go get been at noon and it was now 6 pm and they weren't back yet.

Now Eddie did a lot of things but he never stood Madelyn and their friends up for dinner. Madelyn went to dinner with their friends and everyone knew that she was hurt but she never let on. When she got home the motorcycle was sitting in the front of the house and Eddie was in bed a sleep. But the women with no voice left him sleep and waited until the next day to find out why he stood her up.

Again it was all innocent, and he wasn't gone that long from the house he was visiting. Whoever told her that story was mistaken. Even though Madelyn said do not take that girl on their motorcycle. In her gut she knew what had happen. He had taken her on the motorcycle and he had cheated on Madelyn.

Bruce died that week in hospice care while his wife Carol was in the parking lot having a beer. He wanted her to leave so he could die without her in the room. She was a very dramatic person and caused a lot of scenes in her past so he knew it would be better this way. He loved her no matter what dramatic scenes she caused and he couldn't stop her alcoholism.

Eddie and Madelyn weren't getting along very well after the incident with Carol and Eddie disappearing together and Eddie standing Madelyn up on the dinner date. Madelyn had known what happened and she was so angry that she thought about going to the women's house and confronting her but Carol's husband was dyeing and all the family were there and her hurt was nothing compared to theirs.

Eddie and Madelyn were supposed to go to the funeral but with Madelyn's anger she decided she couldn't go and be embarrassed by the incident that happened just a week before. She waited for Eddie to do his errands and she left and didn't return until the funeral was well over. When he came home he promptly told her how he was embarrassed because she wasn't there at the funeral with him…… She told him there was no way she was going to face the women that he cheated on her with she didn't want to embarrass herself any further and she would never have anything to do with Carol again. It was over for her. Of course Eddie denied the whole thing and it was all her imagination. Eddie was Bruce's best friend. How could he sleep with Bruce's wife when Bruce was dying?

In the light of all that fighting and denying he just couldn't stay away from Carol. She'd call him and ask him to do certain things for her. He would sneak around behind Madelyn's back and do the work Carol asked, and Madelyn would always find out. Eddie must have known that Madelyn wouldn't leave no matter what he did for Carol. Eddie was right she couldn't find her voice and fear of not knowing what she would do if she had no income and no education without him to support her financially.

Madelyn's anger slowly built. She knew she was going to explode if she didn't do something about her relationship with her husband.

She internalized everything that happened between them. Their sex life was nothing by now. Was it her fault she asked herself? She internalized so much that she had a lot of inside physical pain. She started out getting her uterus removed. That was the beginning of her having endometriosis then taking chemo shots that put her into early menopause. That didn't work and she had large fibroids on her ovaries and ended up having her ovaries removed. A complete hysterectomy.

She didn't realize at the time that it was all brought on because of her issues with Eddie not finding her sexually attractive and her first husband always cheating on her.

Her fury built and she thought that she had something wrong with her mind so she sought out Phycologists. Madelyn made appointments and she studied them and they studied her. One that she saw, fell asleep while she talked and the other one she told him that she had just stopped smoking cigarettes and he chain smoking while the room filled with smoke.

Madelyn bought so many self-help books and watched Oprah. When she confronted Eddie about the things she was learning he told her she was watching too much Oprah. What a slap in the face that was.

It wasn't Eddie who was changing it was Madelyn. He was the same man she had married all those years ago and she knew what he did and what he was like when she married him so he made it known to her that he wasn't going to change, that she had to deal with his life style the way it was.

Madelyn prayed the same prayer. "God please make him straighten up or make him leave". It was the same prayer over and over. She wished to start a new life with someone else. Someone who unconditionally loved her. She was looking for that man who would save her, acknowledge her, and appreciate her. She wanted someone taller someone who was a little heavier, someone who would make love to her who didn't fall asleep while making love. She tried to manifest this into her life. To her though it was only a dream that she doubted would ever happen.

Eddie had to leave her… because… she didn't have the strength or the courage to leave on her own.

Madelyn wanted to find the courage to leave, God, she was so miserable with this life. She'd pray" please God show me what to do". It was hard to change what she already knew. It was easy to go back to the life she was used to. She continued to try to find herself with the self-help books. While Eddie tried to convince her that she was crazy, in his own words.

Maybe Madelyn was crazy. She didn't know for sure because of the Phycologists falling asleep and the other one showing her his disrespect while chain smoking when she had told him she quit. They weren't at all interested in helping her. She had to consider all those things that happened. Madelyn was still unhappy even when she tried to be happy.

Madelyn thought about going to school but that fell by the road side. She wasn't smart enough for that. She started getting her daughter to help her work with the computer. It was a secret mission she was bound to accomplish. She didn't want anyone to know. They would just make fun of her especially Eddie who said before she'd never figure out the word processor they had.

Madelyn wrote in her diaries and kept walking or riding her bike when she was stressed out about what was going on in her life. She was lonely and the kids were growing up and she vowed that when they were grown and gone she'd finally leave Eddie. She'd only have to take care of herself then.

Life had a way of presenting things that delayed that process for her.

CHAPTER 23

First Grandson

Madelyn's oldest daughter Camila had a little boy. They called him James. Madelyn's first grandson. She was happy even though no one else was. Camila and Dan were happy even though the baby didn't belong to Dan he seemed to not care and started raising him as his own. Dan even gave him his last name.

Madelyn said she'd watch him while Camila finished school.

Madelyn still went to exercise classes while Dan watched his son. He was so proud of him. Loved him like he was his own.

Madelyn kept him a lot. She loved that little boy and he loved her.

She thought having James and taking on that responsibility changed something in her. She no longer wanted to party. She felt like he was her responsibility because Camila was so young and Madelyn should've been a better mother so in her mind she was responsible to take care of her Grandson.

Camila finished school and graduated with honors and went to work. Madelyn was working to and they had to find a trust worthy babysitter. They were lucky to hire a babysitter who loved Camila and James. She only charged five dollars a day. She babysat Camila when she was a little girl.

Camila and Dan moved in together. Dan started working for

Madelyn's husband as a laborer. Dan loved the work but also loved the benefits which was drinking and doing drugs which made for a bad situation for their relationship. Dan was never home after work until late hours. He drank with the guys after work. Camila being so young didn't want to stay at home and wait on her drunk boyfriend to come home.

She soon became restless but then she became pregnant again. She felt trapped in the relationship and she no longer wanted to be with Dan, pregnant or not. But she stayed at least for a little while.

Again Madelyn felt she had to help with another child. Again she had to repeat the same story of telling everyone that her daughter was pregnant again with another child. They would say she's too young to have another child to hold her back from being the person she should be. Get educated they would say.

She's a whore Madelyn's Mother would say. Madelyn didn't want to deal with anyone's criticism. She had enough of that all her life with her Mother and her ex-husband and her current husband. Madelyn wanted to run away. She just took her long walks and wrote in her diary to keep her own sanity. Madelyn showed how strong she was on the outside but knew she wasn't on the inside. She cried a lot but didn't dare show her pain to the outside would.

CHAPTER 24
Eddie's Friends

Madelyn felt that her husband didn't love her. She didn't realize until much later that he may have loved her but not the way she wanted him too. She was lonely. She didn't want the drinking or the drugs or the Biker Group or the company or the chaos.

The one biker. George, came to their house had a grudge with life and everyone in it. He had to show everyone he was a bad ass. He was stronger, he was smarter and he was a trouble maker. He's the one who told Eddie that Camila was seeing a black boy.

George came right at dinner and sat and ate dinner with them. Madelyn girls by this time had their own lives to live with boyfriends and school work and places to go and people to see. Madelyn couldn't deal with George and his drunken self so she went into the next room to do some sewing. Eddie and George drank and got drunker. The next thing Madelyn heard was a plate being broken in the kitchen and an argument going on. Madelyn sat there thinking it was soon going to calm down but there was a challenge being made by George to go outside to fight. As fights usually go they go outside and talk it out. That didn't happen. She knew that Eddie was too drunk to fight anyone. Before she could get off the couch and go to the door. She looked out the window and Eddie was on the ground and had gotten up with his nose all bloody. It was cold that day. The ground was frozen and when George punched Eddie and he hit the ground it was like hitting concrete.

Madelyn went out the door and ordered George to get out and go home. Eddie and Madelyn went into the bathroom and shut the door and tried to stop the bleeding while Eddie was trying to tell Madelyn what happened and he wanted to press charges against George.

George didn't leave like he was ordered to he opened the door to the bathroom trying to apologize but also blaming Eddie for the fight. Again Madelyn told him to get out he wasn't welcome in their house.

After a while of more arguments and the threat that Eddie told George he was going to jail that Eddie was pressing charges against George, George finally left.

George was a well- known bully. He tried to beat everybody up that he thought was picking on him. George was accused of killing his first wife. They wrecked on his motorcycle and as a result she died. Her family held him responsible for her death. That was a family that couldn't forgive an accident. In turn George held his hatred for her family and turned himself into an alcoholic abuser to others.

In other incidents Madelyn saw how her alcoholic husband disrespected her and their house. Eddie would invite his other friend Danny to their house and they'd proceed to get drunk. She fought so much about him being gone from their home and spending time at the bar that he decided he'd come home but he'd continue his bad behavior at home by drinking and taking the pellet gun and shooting it in the house because it was fun. They took turns shooting at a bottle of polished rocks on top of the cupboard. The glass shattered to the floor and on top of the cupboard and the polished rocks scattered everywhere. Madelyn didn't know what to do. She felt disrespected while Eddie and Danny just thought it was funny and laughed.

He had told her that this is what she wanted for him to be at home instead of at the bars. So, she got her wish. He was home. Things don't always turn out the way we want them to.

Eddie never beat her just verbally abused her into thinking he was the master and she was his subservient wife and telling her she was crazy and how much she had changed since she was seeing her sisters. They were changing her into someone he didn't know. Eddie had a way about him that made her feel like he was taking care of her so she should cut the grass, wash clothes, keep the yard up have dinner by five even if he was out with his friends. Sometimes, he'd pass out and not come home until the next morning. He watched his Mother do all these things so he thought that's what wives do. He was conditioned by his family and he stood by what he believed.

CHAPTER 25

M ore grandchildren came and Madelyn became a busy Grandma. She loved her Grandchildren.

Camila and Dan still together and with now three children. The second one was a girl. Lynn. The third one was another boy. Joe was his name. By then Madelyn was working side jobs of cleaning and babysitting. Dan's mother wanted a baby girl and she loved Lynn. She loved her so much that Lynn stayed there a lot.

Madelyn was pretty much over the drinking and drugs that was in their life. Eddie wanted to go out all the time since the kids could take care of themselves now but Madelyn enjoyed just staying home and babysitting. Eddie didn't like it much so he went out by himself with their friends. He'd end up with the group they mostly hung out with but they had other friends who'd end up with them and most of the time it was with other women. It hurt Madelyn but it was her choice to stay home. She didn't want to drink. It came to a point where her friends no longer wanted to hang out with her either. They wanted to snort coke and drink all night and she'd say to them she didn't understand why they wanted to do those sort of drugs and become addicted.

In the collected crowd of people that they became friends with through the years there were so many of them addicted to crack cocaine. Her closest friends Lizza and her husband became addicted to crack. Another close friend Madelyn became friends with and her husband worked for Eddie had become part of the crowd they also became addicted to cocaine.

Madelyn was the only one who couldn't understand why they wanted this kind of life. Madelyn asked Eddie all the time if he was smoking crack. He always told her no. It was pretty suspicious that they always disappeared into the bathroom at restaurants and at home.

It became obvious to Madelyn that none of her friends wanted to hang out with Madelyn anymore. She had talked with her friend Lizza and had asked her if they were going out one night and Lizza said she would call her if they decided to go out. Madelyn never heard from her so she thought that Lizza and Joe went out together. No big deal she thought but the next day she talked to Camila who was now with another boyfriend who owned a bar and Lizza and their friends where there at the bar and Camila had asked where Madelyn was and Lizza replied "Don't tell her we were here".

Madelyn was hurt but she knew why they hadn't called. Madelyn didn't want to do drugs so instead of having to put up with Madelyn asking why... they just chose not to ask her out anymore.

CHAPTER 26
Working for Mother

Mother wanted her patio fixed. Eddie struck a deal, Eddie and Madelyn needed the money. They had a verbal contract what was to be done and the work began.

Apparently, when the concrete was poured there was no going back and Mother said that was not how she wanted the rain water on the patio to drain. She wanted it the same way it drained before down one hole. Eddie drained it several ways away from the patio and put in several drain holes. She was afraid that the house would wash off the hill during a rain storm with the way he drained it. It was all wrong and that is not what she discussed with him.

She was so distraught over the misunderstanding and they didn't have the money to fix it right then. She made Madelyn's life as miserable as she could because she was miserable. She took every chance she could to call Madelyn out on it and she was going to sue her and Eddie and take everything they had. Madelyn just couldn't even visit her. She hated to anyhow, but she made it even harder to go just to visit and catch up.

The following year Eddie found the money and fixed her patio. It cost more to fix than she paid to have it done. Madelyn didn't care Mother couldn't make Madelyn feel guilty anymore it was done. They learned from that experience. Don't work for relatives.

CHAPTER 27

Alone

Their lives grew further and further apart.

At one point Eddie's Mother said she would ask her tenant to move so Eddie and Madelyn could move in the duplex next to her. At first they said no but as the grandchildren became plenty and they got older they decided at one point to give the oldest daughter Camila and her boyfriend their house to rent. Madelyn and Eddie's house was huge. It became a place where all the grandchildren came and even brought their friends. Madelyn needed space they needed their own lives together they decided to take his Mother's offer.

Camila and her new boyfriend had six kids between hers and his. This offer would help all parties involved. Camila had a house big enough for all the children and Eddie and Madelyn would be alone. The first time in their married life they'd be alone.

That meant that Eddie's Mother was going to ask the girl that was living in the other half of the house to move and his Mother wanted to live in that side of the house and Eddie and Madelyn in the other side.

That was fine with her. Madelyn just needed to get Eddie alone to see if things would get better between them. Madelyn's kids were grown with kids of their own except Christina she had no kids yet but was an adult living with her boyfriend on her own.

Eddie and Madelyn moved but not without problems. Eddie's brother and sister-in-law were not happy that his Mother asked the tenant to leave which was Madelyn's sister-in-law's cousin.

Then there was the carpeting that Eddie's Mother decided to put in their side of the house.

The green eyed monster showed up and they were told by Margaret, Madelyn's sister in law that they weren't happy because they never got new carpet when they lived there. Nothing was said at that time about the cousin that was asked to move.

Eddie and Madelyn moved but it seemed it would never work out for them. Madelyn was lonely. She didn't have kids around to take her mind off of Eddie still being gone everyday all day and into the night. She was really alone now. Nothing changed.

CHAPTER 28

Madelyn was coming home from work one day and she saw smoke up the Run where Camila and Ralph lived. Driving as fast as she could drive to the nearest exit and went toward her old home.

There was no way she could get close enough so she parked and ran part way. Fire Engines, ambulance's and the local news station were everywhere. Their old home stead was on fire.

Just the week before she visited Camila and family and it was a mess inside and out. With that many children all over the place she knew it wouldn't stay the way she'd kept it. In random talk one day (being that she was obsessive compulsive) she thought that she'd wished they'd find a place and move out she had no control over her obsessiveness. Everything had to be in its place and clean and almost perfect. She couldn't stand the fact that it was such a mess. In her mind that was the only way she could keep her sanity was to keep things in order and obsessively clean. She was afraid to have it any other way. That was the only way she had any control over anything in her life. Everything had to be in its place.

All was well with everyone. There were only two family members' home at the time of the fire, Ralph his daughter and Eddie who was fixing the roof at the time the fire started. Ralph's daughter was in the bath tub. The fire started in the front with faulty floor plugs. The doors where open the fire went diagonally to the back bedroom upstairs. The wind was blowing everything in its path caught fire and burned it almost to the ground.

The family moved in with Ralph and Madelyn. Oh goodness. Too many people living in that little house but it was only temporary.

They had a lot of help. Donations came in from everywhere. The people Madelyn worked for gave a lot in clothes, furniture, and money plus the house had insurance.

It wasn't long before the county helped find them a place to live.

Not long after the family moved out Madelyn became sick. Up all night with pains in her right side. She couldn't sleep. The next day Madelyn went to see her Dr. He did tests. It was her gallbladder. She had to have it removed. The procedure was done laparoscopically so she didn't have to stay that long. She wasn't to work for at least three weeks. She came home and lay on the couch and slept most of the time. Eddie stayed home the first day but the next day he had to go to the American Legion and stuff sausage links since now that was his new place to hang out. He left about 10 a.m. and she didn't see him again the rest of the day. She called at 10 pm. She was angry. She's home, freshly had surgery and he thought that stuffing sausage links and friends were more important. She was crazy with jealousy over him and his friends being more important. She cried a lot and prayed that he would both straighten up and be the husband he's supposed to be or just leave.

She called him and he was angry and her being confused about him told him to just stay there if he found that more important when she really wanted him to come home… to just want to come home and spend time with her. He came home they fought. Nothing new. He was drunk so he fought back. That was the only time he fought back when he was drunk. He had a voice then. He passed out and she was left alone hurt and frustrated.

She knew their marriage was coming to an end. She wasn't interested in saving it anymore but she still had that fear of what she would do if they got divorced. There was always going to be an Eddie and Madelyn at least that was her belief. She stayed at home and took care of the kids. She didn't pursue a career. She was cleaning but there wasn't much money in that. She just started out on her own and she didn't find the worth in her work so she charged to little for the work. Eddie and Madelyn had a word processer and Eddie told her she'd never be able to operate it. That she'd never figure it out. It hurt her to the core to think he didn't think she wasn't smart enough. Had he always thought that about her?

She showed him though she got a typing book and learned how to type on it with all the time she had alone she learned how to type. She was so proud of herself. Nobody else but her was proud of her. She didn't let anyone know that she taught myself.

CHAPTER 29

Eddie had stomach problems. Sometimes he'd be in so much pain that he couldn't drink. YaY!!

He still wasn't any fun though when he was sick. He finally went to the Drs. of course she thought he had stomach cancer. Nope it was an ulcer. The kind that could be cured.

He had to go to the hospital. He was given drugs to make him drowsy and then they put a scope down his throat and took a piece of the ulcer out to see if it could be cured with antibiotics. They drove home he loved that feeling. He smoked a joint he bought a twelve pack of beer and went to visit his friends. She knew then that he was a true alcoholic drug abuser. He loved being in that state of euphoria.

The tests came back that he had the kind of ulcer that could be cured with different antibiotics. He took a regiment of different antibiotic s and was cured.

She always thought if something would happen like if the ulcers weren't curable then he'd finally give up drinking and drugs. Or if he'd get a DWI he'd straighten up but he got cured of the ulcers and he has gotten a DUI but that didn't stop him he kept on drinking and driving and doing drugs.

Addiction was something Madelyn didn't understand. She thought that if you loved someone enough that they'd stop the addiction to be with the one you most loved but that is not how addiction works.

CHAPTER 30

As their life moved on Madelyn was very unhappy. Eddie and Madelyn's seventieth anniversary was about to come up and they had made plans with their friends to eat at a Mexican restaurant. Of course Eddie had to go out before their anniversary dinner and get pretty loaded.

Eddie came home took a shower Lizza and Joe picked them up at a spot where they arranged to meet. They met there others friends at the restaurant and had a good time at first. Plenty of drinks were being spread around. Eddie and Joe disappeared to the bathroom during the course of the evening. Eddie came back and was really hipped up and started rolling a joint at the table and Madelyn kept telling him she didn't want to get kicked out of the restraint if someone saw him rolling a joint.

They ended up outside arguing. Madelyn looked up at the moon and saw it was full and she was a believer that things happen on a full moon and they usually weren't good. She decided to try to make up with him and she leaned over and told him let's not fight. He was so angry by then and out of control on cocaine and alcohol that he pushed her. She had heals on and stumbled and fell hitting her face on the ground just in time for Lizza and Joe to walk out and Lizza said "What are you doing on the ground"? Madelyn had gotten up. She had fell out of her heals and as she picked them up and said to her friend Lizza "that son of a bitch pushed me and knocked me down" and as she said those words she wailed the shoes at him and hit him in the eye and he started bleeding. He looked straight at her and said: you'd better not go home". He wanted Joe to call the police... he wanted to file a domestic report on Madelyn. Our lawyer was with them (Joe) and said we both would be arrested if he did that. He didn't care that Madelyn had an instant black eye and a cut on her face from where he pushed her and she hit the side walk. He was always selfish when it came to their anniversary. It was him celebrating their anniversary not them. Everything was about him. He deserved that drink before they went out He deserved the cocaine during their celebration. It was all about him.

They took them to their car. Lizza drove Madelyn home because they didn't trust Eddie to drive her home. Lizza asked Madelyn to go home with her she said no she wasn't afraid of him. She was sober he was high and drunk. Joe dropped Eddie off. Eddie came in the house and started on her that she owed him an apology for being so rude to him in front of his friends. He just kept it up and finally she got down on one knee and said 'Fuck you' and got up. . He came after her as she ran around the table and picked up the wall phone and told him she was calling 911. He went to the phone jack and ripped it out of the wall. She went into the bathroom and shut the door. He kicked it in and on the other side the door hit her in the back. She was calm not afraid and then the fight ended. He passed out and she cried all night and got up early. He had to bid a job it was Saturday and they were supposed to go out that night, just the two of them alone to celebrate but Madelyn wasn't planning on going. She took off just as he was just coming home. He followed her until she stopped and he apologized for his behavior from the night before. They went out that night and ate dinner not hardly saying a word or not talking about what happened the night before and went to a Motel but he passed out from the night before, It took a toll on him and her both. So much energy exerted from that fight. She was so tired of this life. What was she to do? The answer would come later but not without a price to pay and pain to overcome.

So much pain of knowing it was getting to the end of their relationship. That drove a wedge into her heart. Eddie never ever hit her or pushed her down when he was sober. It only happened one time before and he was on drugs that time too.

The next morning they dressed and went to a Football Party at their friend's home. Everything was decorated like a Steeler fan lived there and they were. There were many people there who were Steeler Fan's. Friends of Madelyn and Eddie's.

Eddie and Madelyn had black eyes. Everyone laughed. Madelyn didn't though. She had been laughed at all my life and she took it to heart. It hurt, but she just hid her pain. These people didn't understand what post-traumatic stress disorder was. At the time she didn't know either though. She just reacted like the way she was conditioned to react. Internalize it that was how she kept it together.

Madelyn knew that their marriage was over but she kept praying for him to both change and grow up or just leave her. She didn't have the courage or strength. She was beaten down. She was depressed. She lay on the couch many hours just doing nothing she didn't have the energy to live that kind of life anymore.

She started talking to him about how she felt he said he'd go to a counselor with her. She was happy to think that maybe he'd seen the light. They'd started to see the counselor that she went to when she was married to Jerry at the end of Jerry and Madelyn's relationship. Finally she found someone who listened to her.

They made the appointment. She was excited that finally he would see her side of how she was living with his drinking always coming first and maybe just maybe they could work on their relationship and she could be finally happy....just maybe things would change between them. They went to the appointment but as soon as the Counselor asked the question "Do you think that your drinking has anything to do with the way your marriage is going"? He said "No" Another question was "do you do any drugs"? He said "No"

Counselors were someone you told the truth to but she didn't say anything either for fear that her secret of smoking pot would be revealed. She wasn't perfect either and the fear of personal information coming out was something she didn't want to risk. The embarrassment would be horrific. So, she wouldn't tell on Eddie either. Not yet anyhow...

When they left Madelyn asked him if he thought this was a good idea, he said no. He was only doing it to keep her mouth shut. He didn't believe in counselors and he thought she was watching too much Oprah and that it was Madelyn not him that started changing. Ever since Madelyn went with her sisters on the sister gatherings things began to change. She wasn't the women he first married.

He had never changed in all the time they were together and she knew what he was like when she married him. She became confused and thought he was right... he didn't change, maybe it was her maybe she was the one who needed the counselor not him. What was wrong with her that she was so unhappy? She was so down and so trapped in her own confusion. She wasn't worthy of having a better life. Her Mother was right she was never going to amount to anything.

The couples counseling stopped. Madelyn continued to see the Counselor for her own sanity.

CHAPTER 31

In the future days to come my friend Lizza whom Madelyn loved so dearly decided she was leaving her husband. At this point in both of their marriages their Biker husbands became addicted to crack cocaine. Lizza's husband Joe wasn't in very good health as it was, but he liked his bad behavior. He'd had heart disease and had to get a pace maker/defibrillator put in his chest. That didn't stop him from smoking, drinking, smoking crack, and doing Viagra and all the other pills he had to take to stay alive from his heart disease and that was the part that Madelyn didn't understand ... he didn't want to die. That didn't stop him from living his life to the fullest.

Lizza Joe Madelyn and Eddie were getting ready to go to a biker bash when Joe's heart started beating erratically. He ended up in the hospital for that biker bash.

He was in the hospital until things got better. Joe never let things like that get him down He was always upbeat and determined to live life the way he wanted to. Drinking smoking doing drugs and being wild...

Eddie became addicted to crack. Everyone told Madelyn but she didn't believe them. She had to see it for herself so she tried to find out. She searched everything he had. His truck would have been the place he'd hide things. She couldn't find anything. His brief case was clean of drugs. She followed him to the garage that he often went too, to spy on him, but couldn't see inside to find anything out. He'd come home drunk. Madelyn told him that the rumor was he was doing crack and he always denied that was happening. She could tell something was going on. He had a tick when he was doing crack or cocaine. He had a constant mouth movement that he did. It only appeared when he was high on cocaine. A person knows the facial habits of a person they live with when their facial habits change then there is something different going on in their life. That something was not a good thing.

Personality changes, mouth ticks…come on she knew what was going on she just couldn't find her voice to speak up. She was afraid. So she tucked it inside herself and just wished it would go away on its own.

CHAPTER 32

Lizza left Joe. She moved to Ocean City alone. She met someone and she found a job and she moved in with the guy she was dating. That didn't last long. She then moved in with his sister after the break up. That was a mistake.

Lizza invited Madelyn to the beach to stay with her. It was right after Madelyn's gall bladder surgery and being off work she decided to go. Madelyn wasn't much on driving long distances. She knew she had to overcome some of the fears she had to move forward with her life if and when she decided she'd had enough of Eddie's way of life and decide to move out of his life.

She had fun. She talked about Eddie and how different he was being and what people were telling her about his crack use. Lizza said that's why she left Joe. Too many drugs. Lizza said to Madelyn if you ever decided to leave Eddie she could move there with her. How inviting that sounded but her thought were on my Grandchildren. She loved them so much that she didn't want to leave them.

When she got home Eddie had the same idea he wanted to move to Florida. Their friend Chester invited them to come down to live in Florida. Madelyn didn't want to move. She had the grandchildren and she wanted to stay in Ohio. She cried for weeks.

She prayed that she'd win the lottery so she could stay there or at least travel back and forth to see them. She loved them so much she couldn't imagine being without them. The Universe had other plans for her though. Plans that she couldn't even image was in store for her future.

She knew she wouldn't be any happier there then she was right where she was. Nothing would change. Eddie still would find new friends and stay drunk. He wouldn't be affectionate like she wanted him to be.

Who wouldn't want to move to Florida? Madelyn didn't want too. Madelyn thought she just didn't want to be with Eddie anymore. She was unhappy and knew that a move wouldn't make a difference in their marriage.

CHAPTER 33
One night Stand

Lizza invited her sister Jessica and Madelyn down to the Ocean again. They left one evening and got there about four o'clock in the morning.

Lizza needed a bed and the guy she was dating (a different one) got her one. It came out of a Motel and it was a king mattress. She lived in an upstairs tiny apartment. Donald was on his way over and the guy that was bringing him and the mattress in the truck… broke down. They called another guy to come to their rescue. His name was Stanley. They tried to get the mattress up the stairs to no avail it was too friggin big. Stanley measured the windows to see if they could get it in through the window. No too big. Finally they gave up and Stanley took the mattress home and put it in his shed. He had to get home he kept telling Donald hurry up he had to go home. Lizza and Madelyn thought he had a wife and kids. No, Just a dog. Liza invited them the next day to a bar close to where she lived for drinks since they were so nice to bring the mattress.

That next evening they went to the bar. It was happy hour. Madelyn got so drunk in such a short amount of time and Lizza's sister Jessica got so drunk much drunker than Madelyn that she spent the rest of the evening in the bathroom throwing up. Jessica and Madelyn were not at all drinkers. They both were light weights and got wasted fast. Madelyn wasn't about to get any drunker she was going to have a good time she needed to stop drinking.

I spoke with Donald and Stanley while Lizza was attending to Jessica in the bathroom. I asked their ages. Donald was 32 and Stanley was 29. She laughed... she told them she had kids older than they were. Madelyn was 48 at the time. Only looking to have a good time not looking for a guy. She had one at home and she was pretty sick of him at that point.

Stanley, Madelyn, Lizza and Donald ended up walking our drunk friend Jessica home... boy was she drunk. We got her there, put her to sleep on the floor and decided to catch a cab and go up town. They started out somewhere to have more drinks which Madelyn didn't partake in and she kept telling Jessica to send them home. She didn't of course this was her perspective boyfriend Donald and Stanley was just a friend. Stanley and Madelyn hit it off though. They talked about her marriage how it was falling apart and he talked about his ex-wife and he'd been separated for three years and living at a mobile home park with his Cocker spaniel, Sandy.

They spent the evening talking and ended up dancing and having a good time. The bars called for last call and they finally headed for Lizza's place and Madelyn ended up sleeping with Stanley and by then she was sober. Very Sober!

She'd always had this thought in her head that the next guy she wanted to be with would be taller than herself and a little heavier and he would be very affectionate. She got her wish... that night. She was relaxed and feeling quite good. She'd never had anyone make love to her quit the way Stanley made love to her. It had been a long time since her own husband made love to her.

The next morning he was very affectionate. Played footsies under the table hugged her kissed her and held her. She knew Jessica was watching and she was nervous. It was awkward for her. She hadn't had anyone show that much affection in front of people...Um... Ever!

Jessica and Madelyn had to drive back to their homes that morning. They first took Donald home. Then Stanley. Stanley brought out his dog Sandy so they could meet her then Lizza and Madelyn drove back to her apartment and Jessica and Madelyn got ready to go back home.

She felt so ashamed that she had cheated on Eddie. She had to admit though she enjoyed it. It had been so long since Eddie initiated anything in their relationship. He just didn't have the desire. Madelyn had many thoughts over that. Was it her? Was it that he just liked younger more promiscuous women? Was he gay? He just didn't want to make love with her.

Stanley was so affectionate and so kind and took her feeling into account. But she knew that she would never see him again. He was almost eighteen years younger than her. She just thought he felt safe she was married he didn't have to worry about diseases. One night stand. Oh how she hated that phrase. She felt so cheap. Jessica and Madelyn went home and she had her tail tucked between her legs. She was having guilty moment and the anxiety was out of control.

Madelyn just couldn't quit thinking about her one night stand. It created a big dream in her mind and it was…if only!!

CHAPTER 34

Trial Trip

Eddie and Madelyn made arrangements to fly to Florida since Chester offered them a place to stay. They were supposed to see if they liked it and make a decision to move there.

Of course Eddie had invited our friend Joe to go along and Joe is always late for everything and they missed the plane. They had to get another flight and that meant that Chester wouldn't be able to meet them at the airport and he'd have to make another trip hours later. To Joe and Eddie it was no big deal they could slowly get drunk.

They finally made it. It was intoxicating to see the blue water the sand so white. Hot and Humid. Madelyn got burned of course riding a bike with Betty, and didn't even get to hit the beach. These people didn't like going to the beach. They sat in their screened in porch and watched all the tiny little new born ducks. How cute and the pink flamingos. They were gorgeous. She'd never seen one up close and personal and everything changed when the beautiful Pink flamingo flew down and scooped up the baby chick and flew away with him for supper.

She wanted Eddie and herself to have a romantic evening. She wanted them to just be together. She hadn't been with him for a long time. She had been with Stanley.

It didn't happen between Madelyn and Eddie. Right then and there she knew it wasn't going to be a very good idea to move to Florida. Chester was just another drinking buddy for Eddie any way. Chester didn't love Betty. He was with her for her money. Everyone knew that.

Chester was a good guy. Madelyn liked him a lot but everyone knew that Chester loved money more than he loved Betty. He was a good friend to Madelyn she grew up with him.

They flew back to Ohio and she kept praying for herself to win the lottery. She had that mindset that she was Eddie's wife so she had to go to Florida. But there was that other side of her now that was rebellious and she didn't want to give in to the side that was afraid to say no. She didn't give in though she told him no. She wasn't going he'd have to go alone. He had his threats though "Well if we don't go then we will end up with nothing here, there's no work." She knew what he was saying "Either go or I'll continue doing drugs and hang out with my friends and drink". She didn't want that life anymore. He was gone all the time and his friends were more important and she didn't want to compete with his friends anymore. It would be the same where ever they moved. She was ready for the end of their marriage. She just couldn't step into her courage though. Something held her back. Her good old friend "FEAR".

CHAPTER 35

Secret Admirer

L izza asked her to come back down to the Ocean that she had a secret admirer. It was Stanley. He called her on the phone and they'd talk for hours. Why not, Eddie wasn't home.

Madelyn arranged for Jessica and herself to travel back to the Ocean again. Eddie finally spoke up and said that the last time Madelyn went he was relaxed. He could come home and Madelyn wasn't there to bitch at him for not paying attention to her. He fell asleep any time he felt like it (as if he didn't do that before). In others wards get to steppin... See you later... But no he wanted her to think about it. He wanted her to stay home with him She'd made up her mind she was going to the Ocean to see Stanley.

He had rolled her over that morning and half haphazardly made love to her. She wanted to say no but dutifully went along with it. It was taught through the years that women were subservient to their husbands. That was what she was conditioned to do.

At the Ocean Jessica and Madelyn stayed at Stanley's mobile home. Lizza was in the middle of moving into a double wide with her boyfriend and had no furniture yet so they had no choice but to stay with Stanley but Madelyn didn't mind at all.

Madelyn had a good time. They went out to eat. Drank but didn't get drunk, played pool. She was relaxed and felt good but knew she had to get back home to go to work to explain to her family why she made these out of town trips so often. Time flew by too quickly.

CHAPTER 36
Letter

It had been so long since she had such a relaxing and fun time with any guy that she fell in love with this man who was almost eighteen years younger than herself. She decided not to think about that she'd deal with her feeling later.

Jessica and Madelyn left early on a Sunday morning. Madelyn took her good friend home first. Then Madelyn went home. She knew she'd go home to nobody. Eddie would never stay home to welcome her home. He never did... so why would he this time.

Not to her surprise nobody was home but there on the stove, missed spelled words and all was a Dear Madelyn letter, it said" I'm finally giving you what you've wanted for a long time. I've moved out. I love you but its better this way. We aren't happy together". Love Eddie.

There was a lot more to say but she couldn't remember what all of it said. She was in shock. She cried but laughed at the same time. Something that she dreamed of... either straighten up or she'd wished he'd leave her. After eighteen years of manifesting, it came true. Only at that time she had no idea about manifestation. It was probably called something else then. She just knew she had a bigger dream than what Eddie wanted and wished and prayed for it for a long time. It became confusing at times through the years by changing her mind thinking that things would get better and sometimes they did.

So, he took all his belongings. Everything was gone that belonged to him. Everything that belonged to her was there except a couple hundred dollars in one dollar bills that she had saved. He had left three hundred.

Of course, she cried for days weeks and months. Twenty years out the window. She had a job but only made forty dollars a day. Madelyn had a house now that was empty. She'd lost her big house to fire. Eddie spent all the money they had in saving from the house fire insurance for his payroll and gave her the excuse that the people that he worked for wouldn't give him a draw on the job until it was done. She believed him. She did get a used Lincoln Continental from an auction with some of the insurance money. Eddie thought she'd like it. It's what he wanted, not what Madelyn wanted.

Of course Eddie got another truck with a nice cap for the back of it and spent the rest on cocaine or crack.

By this time Madelyn had quit all drugs even pot. She had stopped smoking cigarettes when her Mother was diagnosed with cancer.

Now that old desire was back. She was stressed out about not having a good job. Not planning her retirement a little better. She'd go to the property that Eddie and Madelyn bought from a crack addict. She'd buy a pack of cigarettes and a bottle of White Zinfandel wine and just cry. She wanted this change in her life but now that she had it she didn't know how to handle it even though she knew she wasn't going back to what she already knew. She was tired of being miserable. Her friend was back ...FEAR!!!

CHAPTER 37
Eviction Notice

Madelyn worked every day. She didn't eat much. She had to pay the bills that were left to pay.

After Eddie had left Eddie's brother and sister -in -law took over the power of her Mother in laws life. Her Mother –in-law had talked about everything until one day Madelyn had mentioned she was going to help her daughter after she had the baby. Her Mother in law said to Madelyn that she didn't think that her other son would let that happen. Madelyn was already depressed and confused about what she was going to do and she said to her Mother in law that she may let them tell her what to do but they weren't going to tell Madelyn what to do in her own home. But Madelyn had forgotten this was not her home it was their home and her husband had left her and she had no say as to what was going to go on in her own place that she lived in.

Madelyn went out to dinner with her daughter Christina and her husband and while she was gone Madelyn came home to a voice message on her home phone from her brother-in- law saying that Madelyn had to move out and to stay away from her mother-in -law because her blood pressure was getting out of control because of Madelyn. That in between finding a place to live, to pay rent and Madelyn needed to stop spreading rumors around about Eddie, that he was on crack. It was ruining his reputation. The message went on to say that Madelyn had sisters that she could move in with and it was a better then what Madelyn had given their cousin who used to live on the other side when Madelyn made her move out. The Cousin had to live in her car until she found a place to live... Wait What? Madelyn didn't make her move that was her Mother- in -law that wanted Madelyn and Eddie to move there so Madelyn could take her to the Doctors, cut the grass, keep the yard cleaned up and clean the porches. She wanted to see more of her son. So how's that Madelyn's fault?

Madelyn also found a letter under her door along with the voice message. Ok, wasn't hearing it enough instead of writing it to. At the end of the voice mail there was one comment that her brother in law made that if Madelyn had have been in his presents, she would have definitely slapped him and probably went to jail. He said "Get you and your scumbag children out of my Mother's house". It certainly hurt. This was my brother- in -law who I've known for many years and couldn't stand up to his wife or anyone else for that matter. That's why he wrote the letter and left the voice message.

Madelyn got blamed for a lot of stuff that was going on in their minds that just wasn't true. Madelyn thought that Eddie made his own reputation by smoking crack. She finally found out for sure Eddie smoked crack... One evening while she was home a knock came on her door. It was a fellow asking if Eddie was around that he had found Eddie's brief case in the street. Madelyn told him that Eddie no longer lived there and he showed her the brief case. It had been run over and was pretty smashed. Madelyn took the brief case and searched it for whatever he may have had in it and there it was the proof she had not believed was true but there it was a "Crack Pipe".

Madelyn had no other choice but to move she had signed a paper when they first moved in to take the house out of Madelyn's name. Her Mother in law had put the house in Eddie's and Madelyn and the brother and sister in laws name in case something would happen to her. She had had a stroke about five years before and thought that she would have another one and she had to get her affairs in order so she transferred the house over to her children. When Madelyn and Eddie moved in her Mother in law was so afraid that one of her daughter in laws would get greedy and put her in the nursing home so Madelyn decided she didn't want to be put into that situation so she opted out of the signing.

Madelyn never did talk to her Mother in law again until just before she moved. Eddie told her she could have everything so she decided to sell the riding lawn mower. She sold it to her Mother in law. Madelyn needed the money since she had to leave the house.

She saw a lawyer and he advised her she had no rights to the house. The lawyer hated Joe (our old lawyer). He tried to get Madelyn to tell him everything she knew about Joe. He wanted to get Joe disbarred. Madelyn was still loyal to her friend and didn't repeat the fact that he also was a crack head.

Madelyn took her time getting things together and packing everything up in boxes. She only saw her mother-in-law once after the message the letter and selling the lawn mower to her when she went over to get the money her Mother in law asked where she was going to go and Madelyn told her that she was going to sleep in the car like Madelyn made the other tenant that lived there. Her Mother in law told her that wasn't true and where would Madelyn get that idea?

Hummm!! Such lies were told just to hurt her... Madelyn knew her Mother in law really didn't know the difference between a lie and the truth but neither did either one of her sons or her daughter in law for that matter.

There were a few lies told through the years. When Madelyn confronted her Mother in law on those lies she'd hang up on Madelyn and say she wished she were dead. Madelyn knew she had to make up with her. Eddie would make her life miserable over his Mother. She was afraid of what he would do but this time she didn't care about his Mother.

CHAPTER 38

Truth

Madelyn cleaned the house that Eddie moved to. It was Joe and Lizzas house but Lizza didn't live there anymore. She needed the money and when she went there to clean one day there they were... Eddie's new girl and Eddie sleeping on the couch and the house was in shambles. There were beer cans everywhere. Spoons that were black from cooking coke to make crack. Eddie got up and was still drunk from the night before and he swore they weren't doing anything. He wasn't smoking crack. She picked up a spoon that was burned from cooking the cocaine and she said "what's this"? Eddie took the spoon and said he doesn't get addicted to anything and licked the spoon. They argued and friends came in. My friend Shannon and Liza's daughter came to the house. Liza's daughter kept making excuses that they all had been to a concert and they crashed there. It was a work day for goodness sakes everybody was supposed to be at work. Madelyn was upset and Eddie begged her to let him come home so he could get some sleep she told him no and left.

Madelyn went home and started thinking. Eddie had her credit card and she needed to find out if he used it. He had charged a motel room on her credit card so he could sleep with that girl. She couldn't take anymore. She had finally broke and decided she had to call her phycologist. Maybe she could help her through this emotional break down she was having.

She saw her therapist and told her what she had found and then her therapist gave her this advice "move to the beach away from this hurt and your children even if it was for a little while to figure everything out". Madelyn had told her that her children didn't want her to go. Her therapist said to her God forbid that anything would happen to you then what would your children do? They'd learn to live without you but this way you'd still be in touch and be able to visit. That's when Madelyn gave herself permission to move away from the chaos in her life. God gave her all the signs but she still had to have permission to go.

Madelyn had made a decision to move to the beach with her friend Lizza who had asked her long ago to move with her. She had three choices. She could move in with one of her children or she could move in with one of her sisters or move with her friend at the beach. Even though the beach is the best and easiest decision it still wasn't an easy decision to leave her children and grandchildren.

She now had to break the news to her children and grandchildren that she was moving to the beach. She didn't want to live with the kids or move with her sisters. She made a choice to move away from that town. She needed to make a fresh start. Of course that choice was hard and there were a lot of tears and second guessing herself. How could she leave her family? All she has ever known was there in that little town. She was overwhelmed with emotions. Lizza wanted her to move in with her. She'd be near Stanley also. Then Stanley asked her to move in with him. A new beginning was about to start and new feeling of anxiety that Madelyn had to learn to deal with. She had to keep reminding herself that her children were grown they had lives of their own and it was time for Madelyn to find out who Madelyn was and what new things she could conquer. She was going to find out who she really was.

Stanley came to Ohio to meet her daughters. First off he made a bad impression. He brought beer and drank. The girls knew how much their Mother hated drinking and he started bragging about renting a motel room with mirrors on the ceiling. Oh my GOSH. She was simply embarrassed. You don't tell a Mother's children that you're taking their mother to a motel with mirror. What was she thinking when she decided to introduce her boyfriend to her children. There it was again. She was so conditioned to always hiding things that she thought was inappropriate around her children. She was a full grown women for goodness sakes couldn't she do what she wanted for once without answering to anyone about her behavior.

Madelyn's kids were afraid that something would happen to her. Their Mother was about to move 450 miles away, with a man she didn't even know and one friend who they thought was a bad influence on their Mother. It was a big step for all of them. The lesson was hard but necessary.

CHAPTER 39
Packing

M adelyn took her time packing and boxing and separating things and cleaning while all the time just crying. It seemed to be non- stop. She still went to her private cleaning jobs knowing that she would have to tell them that she was moving and they'd have to find someone else. She had to save all the money she could to get a good start where she was going. She had one credit card so she had to at least pay minimum payments to keep her credit building to good credit. She wanted the reputation of having good credit and a job.

Eddie came to the house one day just to stop. He saw the girls there so he thought it would be ok. It was getting cooler out so she made Chili. He came in like he lived there and she asked him what he was doing he asked if he could stay for dinner she said yes. The next thing Madelyn knew Eddie had made himself comfortable on the couch... sleeping. Dinner was served Eddie got up and ate and the girls all left except one granddaughter. Madelyn asked when Eddie planned on leaving. He said in a little while and she left to take her granddaughter home. When she got back there he was laying on the couch. He left long enough to go to the store to buy candy. His favorite thing to do was lay on the couch and eat candy and sleep. She asked again when he was leaving he begged to sleep on the couch. She told him she had to sleep on the couch because the upstairs furniture was gone she'd given it away. He said he had no money and he couldn't handle the partying out at Joe's house. He wanted to come home. She stuck to her decision to not take him back. He'd hurt her for the last time and she knew if they'd go back together it would be the same life all over again. She'd be unhappy and be stuck again. It would have been so much easier to go back to what she already knew but she was determined this time to start fresh. Her soul was calling out to her to move forward not backward. She was scared, but so determined to change her life for the better. She was very excited to make this change.

She left the refrigerator and couch one spoon, one fork, one plate, one cup one knife one kettle one towel. Nothing else. Madelyn moved in October 1999.

She was too say the least...anxious and wondered if she had made a mistake. She missed the grandchildren the most. She interacted with them all the time before she moved. It brings tears to her eyes as she thought about leaving them all. She reasoned with herself that this was the best thing for everyone. It was time to let them live their lives and not have her interfere. They had their own journey to live.

Madelyn took some advice from one of her clients that she cleaned for. The client told her to give it a chance. Don't let the home sickness take Madelyn away from something that could be wonderful. Madelyn took her advice and didn't go back home where she was being called to every day. Every day she thought about going back. She was homesick.

She almost left a few times She found a job. The only thing she knew how to do was clean. She applied at motels and got a cleaning job. She also got a job at a place that rented Condos. For a while she had two jobs. That was too much and soon quit one job that paid the least and went full time at the Condo Rental place where she cleaned and did various jobs. It expanded her knowledge about business. Her thoughts were to maybe someday become an entrepreneur in her own business.

CHAPTER 40

Learning How Too Cope

Stanley was good to Madelyn. He made Candle lit dinners and she thought she'd died and gone to heaven. She'd never had that happen, only in her dreams.

There was just one problem... she missed her kids that was without being said, but the bigger problem was Stanley drank. He wasn't an all week drinker just a weekend drinker and he drank a lot. Madelyn worked sometimes until 8 pm on Friday's and Stanley got off work at noon and started drinking and by the time Madelyn had gotten to the bar he'd be good and drunk but she couldn't tell it. She'd drink her usual two and be done. They'd go home and he'd pass out and have a big headache the next day he'd lay on the couch. He often would have a headache so bad that he had to go to the bedroom with all the blinds pulled and stay in the dark.

It took Madelyn awhile to get accustomed to a different life. Her last marriage influenced this relationship. She was used to being alone because Eddie was never home but Stanley was home all the time. Madelyn was used to cleaning all the time but she couldn't there. The mobile home was really small.

The weekends were boring and she hated watching Stanley sleep. Then his boss sent him away to work in Cape May New Jersey. He didn't come home on the weekends so she visited him. This went on for a while and she became really bored. She had no kids to take care of now. He was away and she was really alone. She went out with her friend Lizza but her life was filled with her boyfriend or working. Madelyn didn't really like to drink much. She'd do her usual two and was ready to go home.

She finally told Stanley that she didn't come here to be alone again so he told his boss that he wanted to stay close to home. His boss brought him home but was upset that Stanley didn't want to go out of town. Madelyn encouraged Stanley to move forward with his life he wasn't getting paid for what he was worth and there was no room to move up in the job. He was being put on the back burner while the boss hired other people to do what Stanley could do. So, Stanley found another job.

Stanley continued on with his drinking though. It was something she just didn't want in her life so she considered leaving and being homesick was almost making her decision for her.

One day out of the blue Stanley decided to stop drinking to see if the headaches would stop. He still got the headaches but not as often or severe. He totally stopped drinking. Madelyn was happy with that decision. His moods became better. His headaches weren't as severe.

The headaches were caused from allergies and apparently something in the beer caused him to have severe blinding headaches.

She still missed home, the kids were not financially able to visit. Stanley's mobile home was too small to have visitors especially with the size of her family.

They managed to visit with a bunch of them all at once. They slept everywhere and anywhere and they brought friends. Stanley was not happy. He was alone for three years before Madelyn came in to his life.

Stanley is very out spoken. He doesn't think before he speaks sometimes and that gets him into trouble with Madelyn and with others who are within ear shot. Stanley hurt a lot of feeling with some of his out spoken remarks. Madelyn was the kind gentle person who would never say anything out of the way to hurt anyone. She'd hurt herself first before she'd hurt someone else's feelings even if they deserved it.

She was in fear of getting repercussions and her Mothers words would ring in her ears. "You are to be seen not heard." Conditioning "she called it being brain washed.

Madelyn and the girls and grandchildren would go to the beach and Stanley stayed home. They stayed away as long as they could as to not come home to hear Stanley remark and be critical of everyone. They all stayed just for the weekend and that was enough for Madelyn to always stand guard and fix the critical remarks made from Stanley. Madelyn made the decision to talk with Stanley about his verbal assaults on her family.

Stanley was still good to her. He told her every day how beautiful she was and how easy it was to love her. At first she used to say sure you're just saying that. Madelyn saw herself in the mirror everyday she knew she wasn't beautiful. Who was he trying to kid? Saying how easy she was to love. If that were true why was she divorced two times? But every day he just kept telling her how beautiful she was and thanked her for being in his life. He opened doors for her, he helped with laundry and he did dishes. She wondered how long this would go on. She thought to herself "is this man for real" Stanley became the man that was her rock. He stood by her through every situation that became hard to deal with. They became best friends. They could talk about everything and anything. Except her children.

Stanley still had that outspokenness about him and it got him into trouble sometimes but he tried to keep his mouth shut and think before he said anything to anybody. Sometimes he'd say things to her as though those children were not hers. He often criticized her children and grandchildren and the Mother that she was she stood up for them. Her love for her children was unconditional. Unlike her Mother.

CHAPTER 41

Eight Years Later

S tanley's bosses' sister-in-law passed away and she was a twin to Stanley's boss's wife. She was a good friend as well. It was total chaos during that time. The boss's wife was devastated that her twin sister had passed. Stanley was the supervisor then so he was trying to do a lot of work for his boss since he had to deal with his wife's sister's death. Stanley tried to step onto a scaffolding and ended up falling onto the ground and broke his back which he didn't know it at the time. He was just in a lot of pain but laid there and didn't want anyone to call an ambulance. They all thought he hit his head.

Madelyn was at home cooking supper and Stanley called and asked her what she was doing. She asked him the same question. He said that he was just laying around in the hospital calling her. What?? What happened? He said he fell but he thought everything was fine just waiting for x-rays. The next phone call he had asked her to come over and get his truck they were flying him to the trauma center. His back was broken and they didn't want him to move around the bone was splintered and it may cut into his spine and paralyze him.

Madelyn had by then started a partner business with her friend and stayed at home while his Mother visited him until the weekend. Madelyn went up and brought him home in a body cast that was removable. He wanted no surgery and wanted no pain killers. Stanley was down for about three to four week. The Doctor released him but told him not to work but Stanley couldn't sit still and went back to work.

Madelyn had brought some of her grandchildren to visit for a few weeks. They helped wait on Stanley while he was down.

Stanley came to her after he became able to work and asked her to marry him. She was surprised. It had been eight years since she left her home town. She had been home sick for seven years and decided that this was where she was supposed to be.

Stanley and Madelyn were married almost exactly to the day eight years after she entered his life. A small ceremony by the justice of the peace. A small gathering of her family but not all and his Mother and Step Father and two friends that stood up for them, his boss Charley and wife Alexis.

CHAPTER 42
Finding Madelyn

Through the years of being abused by her Mother and the husbands in her life she found the reason she had to live through those troubling times. She had to find out who she was and what she was capable of.

Her Mother was abusive and Madelyn hated her. Her Mothers voice stayed in her head even after she had passed. She didn't know she had been brained washed in to believing she was worthless. She thought she was ugly and everyone else had more worth then herself. Everything that happened to her she believed she deserved it and that no one loved her. No one protected her from the sexual abuse she received and she didn't tell anyone who abused her. She felt there wasn't any use because not even her parents protected her when she revealed her first encounter with almost being raped.

Madelyn was a kind and gentle soul. She didn't want to hurt anyone. She took a lot of abuse to protect her children. She didn't want them to endure the same abuse she went through. Even though they went through worse than she did. Madelyn was a very low self-esteem person and she passed that onto her children without even knowing that she did.

Madelyn learned through reading and webinars and self-help

books and a sister with a big heart all that happened to her was all in God's plan to move her forward to where she is supposed to be. She found herself to be one of the good people in life. She was blind to all this as though she lived her life not knowing or understanding what abuse was or what anxiety was. She thought that it was a natural part of life so she stayed quiet and reserved burying all thoughts that this treatment was normal.

Madelyn is beautiful inside and out. She cares about everyone and they care about her. She always thought that people said nice things to her just to be nice not because they were true. When it was repeated over and over again to her that she was easy to love and she was kind and gentle and she was beautiful she finally started to believe it.

Madelyn's life experiences every single event contributed to who she is. She could see life and what she was good at once she got out of her head and started realizing that it wasn't her Mother that held her back… it was herself. She didn't realize she had anxiety. She didn't realize she was being abused. She thought it was just the way things were.

Things started popping up in her life about writing a book. Madelyn started watching webinars on writing books. She went to her local library to see an Author talk about writing books and what should be done to get the book started. It scared her just to think about how much money it would cost (a belief that was drilled into her growing up that there wasn't enough money) and everything she'd have to know and learn and the old belief came back that she couldn't learn. She always had a phobia about tests and learning. That same voice kept telling her how dumb she was and that she'd fail at this and how ashamed she'd feel if she'd failed or what If it was not interesting just a boring life that she'd led as a child. She sank into denial that she just knew she couldn't write a book. As she kept telling herself all those what ifs and finally she decided to hide it again deep down inside herself and never bring it up again. She wouldn't listen to the inner voice that tried to move her forward she just kept shoving it back down. That voice kept calling to her through different webinar's. Through listening to Wayne Dyer, Louise Hays, Reid Tracey, just to name a few that kept showing up in her internet searches. Write the book they kept saying. Don't die with the book inside of you.

Then the offer came through Hay house to sign up to write a book and then they called and she ignored the phone calls she was so afraid. How could she do this?

Then one day she answered the call. She kept making excuses to the person who called her from Balboa Press. She just kept them at bay. Life kept her busy though. She worked and took on grandchildren to raise and great grandchildren. That same subject kept coming up though. People kept telling her she had a good book inside of her.

She finally came to a decision one day when she was reading an article. The article said so what if you fail at least you got it out there and it is no longer inside of you.

Her secret would finally be out. She hated her Mother when she started the book but as days weeks and years went by she learned a lot about herself and how to forgive her Mother and Father for how she was brought up. They only treated her how they were raised and the times they lived in.

Everything she knew was all they taught her. The abusive part she didn't believe was the right way to raise children so she had to start out from scratch. She also found out that there is no written code to raise children and there are no perfect parents. They all make mistakes and when those mistakes are made you learn to forgive yourself and not to hang on to the guilt.

We are all born perfect but learn some bad habits some good habits as we get older and carry those imprinted hurts or beliefs whatever you want to call them with us through our lives which can cause pain or addictions because we hang onto them. Learn to let that pain go.

Madelyn hung on to her pain for many years. She abused herself by thinking constantly about how she hated her Mother and that was a sin according to the church that taught her it was wrong and she would go to hell. She was lost for a very long time and when someone told her she had to love herself she thought it was selfish to love yourself first. Madelyn's brain didn't work like most people's brain. She was easily confused. She was easily convinced that whatever the abuser wanted her to do or say she readily did it because she looked so hard for that approval. Something she never got from her Mother.

Madelyn is still searching for all the answers. Still learning about herself. She is still afraid at times. She has many phobias to overcome but as the days go on she is willing to go the extra mile to find out more about herself.

Her life with her present husband was manifested through years of praying and she is happy with him. They are best friends.

There is so much more to tell that she has gone through just to prove she was honest and reliable. She didn't make promises she couldn't keep she kept most of them. She now knows she is a wonderful wife, friend, sister, Mother, grandmother and great grandmother. She also knows that it's none of her business what other people think of her.

TO ALL THAT READ THIS BOOK

To all that read this book you don't have to do this to yourself. We are all perfect the way we are. We all make mistakes and it's ok as long as you forgive yourself and change your thoughts from negative to positive and learn from the lessons that are presented to us as we move forward in life.

Know that the Universe has got your back and have Faith that things will work out. Know that you are love and that you are loved. You are a part of everything beautiful on Gods earth.

Love to all that reads my book. Learn from your mistakes and move on. Don't hang on to the pain.

Love
Wilomino Pearl

Printed in the United States
By Bookmasters